FROM THE HANDS OF DELILAH TO THE ARMS OF SAMSON

BECOMING THE JEWEL HE DESPERATELY NEEDS

FROM THE HANDS OF DELILAH TO THE ARMS OF SAMSON

BEING THE MAN SHE ESSENTIALLY DESIRES

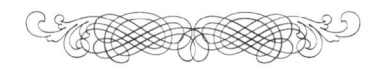

MO STEGALL

THE COMPLETE GUIDE TO HEALING HIS HEART | RESTORING HIS MANHOOD | EMPOWERING HIS SOUL

ANTDREREN
publishing
GROUP INC.

LOS ANGELES | ATLANTA | CHARLOTTE

All rights reserved. No part of this book may be reproduced or transmitted in any form or by any means, electronic or mechanical, including photocopying, recording or by any information storage and retrieval system, without written permission from the author, except for the inclusion of brief quotations in a review.

Unless otherwise noted all scriptures used are from King James, New Living Translation and NIV Version of the Bible.
Includes bibliographical references.

For more information, contact info@antdrerenpublishing.com
www.antdrerenpublishing.com
From The Hands Of Delilah To The Arms Of Samson
Copyright © 20012 by Antdreren Publishing Group Inc.

First Edition, 2012

Publisher's Cataloging-in-Publication Data
Library of Congress Control Number: 2012916066

Stegall, Mo, 1974

From the Hands of Delilah to the Arms of Samson / Mo Stegall
ISBN-10:0615690823
ISBN-13:978-0-615-69082-7

Interior Design by I Can Be Foundation Inc. Graphics Division
Editing & Proofing: Saadia James & Antwione Griffin
General Editor: Donya LaRousa
Consultant Editor: Tiffany Stegall
Prepared for Publication by Antdreren Publishing Group Inc.
Cover Design: I Can Be Foundation Inc. Graphics Division
Antwione Griffin
Printed in the United States of America

PRAISE FOR
FROM THE HANDS OF DELILAH TO THE ARMS OF SAMSON

Mr. Stegall has birthed a very important book that will help us as a people go to the next level. This book is very important because it's tackling issues that many brush under the rug. Mr. Stegall has proven that he's been given a message that the world should hear and this book is proof of that. Because of his insight and wisdom, this book will reach areas and points that other books around this topic have not. This is definitely a book we need!

-**Tony A. Gaskins Jr.**
Author, Celebrity Life & Relationship Coach

This wisdom-based book written to encourage the explanation and exploration of negatives in men and relationships that have established unconscious patterns and replication in succeeding relationships is a must have and a must read. Readers will gain insight from Mo's knowledge and with sincere application of the concepts herein, will experience happier, healthier relationships and consequently happier marriages.

-**Yvette Williams**
National Recording Artist, Producer, Songwriter

The laws of supply and demand play an integral role in navigating the road of relationships. Proverbs suggests, "who can find a faithful man" and "who can find a virtuous woman?" In this treatise, Mo Stegall unveils practical truth through God's Word to help you discover the treasure that is within you. This provocative and powerful book is sure to enlighten, empower, and encourage you.

- **Eddie Connor**
Author and Speaker, www.eddieconnor.com

This book is a great institution of healing, restoration, empowerment, and full of information, challenging questions and practical applications to uplift men and women from the obscurity of self-imposed sanctions allowing true redemption versus simply pulling off the Band-Aid and being left exposed.

-**Tina DeVeaux**
CEO, Xtreeme Media

When Mo Stegall speaks...*The Wise Listen*. This book is stunningly powerful. It is an honor to commend this book to every person who longs for *The Uncommon Life*. After reading it *You Will Never Be The Same*.

-Dr. Mike Murdock
Author, Senior Pastor, The Wisdom Center

This book is long over-due. It's a "Manhood Manual" making a clarion call for all men to transcend *every* trial, tribulation, or past hurt, and take their rightful place as the head of every household. This is a blue print for becoming what every wife desires and son will emulate—a man who's strong as steel *and* smooth as velvet.

-Walter Kasmir, PhD,
Neurotherapist and Peak Performance Coach at Lake Norman Neuro Feed Back and Peak Performance Center Mooresville, NC

This book is timely and very necessary! Men and women across the globe will be emphatically empowered by this wonderful gem. It gives the reader an in depth understanding of what men desperately need from women and what women essentially desire from men. It lends a unique voice and innovative perspective and Mo Stegall has given us a jewel that speaks volumes!!!

-Tia Dantzler
Celebrity Makeup Artist

Mo Stegall is on a mission to bring healing and understanding to both men & women by exposing the pitfalls that destroy many relationships. As a man who has a desire to truly restore men and empower women, he uses biblical principals and practical steps that equip the reader with a road map to building the type of relationship God ordained.

-Roshonda Payne
Editor-in-Chief, The Savvy Sistah

"The Jewel Expert - Mo Stegall has out done himself with this book. This book gives you access inside the innermost thoughts & feelings of a man you will discover things that your man would probably never open up to tell you it will definitely educate you on what we really need and desire from our mate and what God has ultimately called you to do.

-Kelly Cole "The Generator"
CEO Prime Time Marketing, Author, Speaker

Dedication

To my loving father Lee E. Griffin for all that he has given me.

To all the men and women across the globe who are seeking consequential relationships with purpose.

Acknowledgements

What a journey this project has taken me on. I thank God for entrusting me with such a delicate assignment. I want to thank all of those who had a hand in helping me complete this project and those who did not want me to explore this subject matter.

To my entire family, friends, associates, contributors and endorsers thank you.

To all of you who have purchased this book thank you. To every retailer, distributor, publishing house and wholesaler thank you for carrying this book.

God Bless all of you and I pray that this book is as much a blessing to you as it was to me while writing.

Contents

Foreword xi

Introduction xiii

PART ONE: HER BEAUTY

Chapter 1 What Gotcha 17
Chapter 2 The Curves of Social Media................................... 26
Chapter 3 Fishing for Fool's Gold 33
Chapter 4 Daddy Created This 36
Chapter 5 Broke, Sick, Lonely 43

PART TWO: HER VOICE

Chapter 6 Honey Lips 51
Chapter 7 Lying to Live: Decepticons 58
Chapter 8 Listen & Respond 64

PART THREE: HER FLATTERY

Chapter 9 The Poison In Her Heart Will Kill You 73
Chapter 10 The Bodyguard 76
Chapter 11 The Black Hole 78
Chapter 12 What Is She Really Attracted To? 81
Chapter 13 Slippery When Wet 90

PART FOUR: HER TOUCH

Chapter 14 Her Hand | His Heart 96
Chapter 15 Entrapment of the Cookie Jar............................ 100
Chapter 16 She'll Never Be More Than Your Mistress 106
Chapter 17 Laying In Her Lap... 113

PART FIVE: HER LOVE

Chapter 18 The Glass Half Empty 121
Chapter 19 What The Wife Refuses The Girlfriend Won't 126
Chapter 20 What's Missing?... 133
Chapter 21 Matters of the Heart.. 137

Chapter 22 No Love Given No Love To Give 141
Chapter 23 Love Jones 148
Chapter 24 Thrill Of Victory 153
Chapter 25 Hiding The Hurt Hinders The Healing 155
Chapter 26 Residue In The Relationship 159
Chapter 27 Conflicts of Interest 162

PART SIX: HER MISSION

Chapter 28 Where Does This Road Lead? 168
Chapter 29 Not Sick But Single 173
Chapter 30 Marriage Material 176
Chapter 31 Marrying Jezebel 186
Chapter 32 Just Being A Man 191
Chapter 33 The Short Game 197
Chapter 34 Quantity Versus Quality 201
Chapter 35 Why Single Women Date Married Men 204

PART SEVEN: HER JEWELS

Chapter 36 The Substitute? 219
Chapter 37 Just An Option Not A Priority 223
Chapter 38 Diamond Mine or City Dump? 226
Chapter 39 Cycle Of Acceptance 230
Chapter 40 Not Ready 233
Chapter 41 Good Enough To Be The Roommate 237
Chapter 42 You Want To Matter! 240
Chapter 43 Becoming The Treasure Hunter 247
Chapter 44 The Jewel Expert 254
Chapter 45 The Closer 264
Conclusion 273

Foreword

Many men share their *hurt*, but far too few share their *heart*. Many willingly share their *love,* yet few are willing to share their *lives*. Many share their *passion*, but few their *person*.

In his new book, *From the Hands of Delilah to the Arms of Samson,* author Mo Stegall embarks on a journey that constrains men to confront the common trepidation of "full disclosure." Using the familiar narrative of *Samson and Delilah,* or *Strength and Deceiver* (my own appellation), Stegall makes the compelling presentation that sharing hurt doesn't make a man *vulnerable*. Rather, it makes him *valuable*. As the hurt man shares his heart, he is then healed and effectively able to lend his hand to help another who has been similarly harmed.

The Samson narrative chronicles the all too familiar downward emotional trajectory of the unsuspecting man who shares all of himself with a person of evil intent. In lieu of helping him, lady Delilah sets out to destroy Samson with his own secrets. Samson, once a victor, becomes a victim. Once notorious for his strength, he succumbs to the disingenuous embrace of lady Delilah, the delectable, desirable diva, infamously memorialized for her devious deception. Quite naturally, issues of trust and hurt ensue. It is against this kind of backdrop that many men become reclusive stoics, too afraid to open up to spouses, family or friends. They opt, instead, for suppression and avoidance. While these defense mechanisms are used as safeguards against external

pain, they eventually are nothing more than actuators of self-cannibalism, whereby the essence of the man's life is eaten away by the un-reconciled issues of his inner self.

In this fresh literary offering, Stegall helps men all over the world to break this vicious cycle of pain and emotional censorship. Sit back and enjoy his poignant observations. Embrace his prudent remedies to this age-old issue. But I must warn you—he may put a finger on some really sticky places in your life.

My prayer for every reader is that he is completely healed and positioned to help facilitate the healing of others. While it's true that "hurt people hurt people," it's also true that "healed people heal people!"

-**Kevin Bond**

Kevin Bond

Multiple Grammy-Award Winning
Producer & Author

Introduction

Keep Running: The Race Is Far From Over

The journey we encounter from the quiet halls of the hospital after delivery to the lives we develop as adults seems like a Hollywood movie at times taking us from one extreme to the next. Building any type of relationship takes dedication, patience, and a solid commitment to growing, but it is those relationships that we encounter in life that shatters our very being that are the most difficult ones to adjust to.

No one is immune to hurt and heartache and I have searched for what seems an eternity to identify why I have certain characteristics, habits, and actions when it pertains to various people. I have concluded that my low level of trust for people is due to the repeated hurt I have suffered and the empty feelings of abandonment by those that were close in my circle of friends, family or professional affiliates.

When I was a young man, I discovered my love for Track & Field through my local church and the feeling of getting out on the track and racing towards the finish line to a thunder of applause and cheers allowed me to escape life's issues and feel alive and loved. Many of us are in search today of the seemingly ever eluding batch of hugs, appreciation, and sincere love we desire. Your quest for acceptance is blinding at times to the revolving door of redemption and restoration. Many men have roamed the earth in search of an escape route while hiding the true heart of their issues relinquishing any resolution to healing; I offer you a remedy that will touch the essence of your inner most hurt and heal those troubled waters that may prohibit you from receiving true freedom. God has given every man a gift and that is LOVE!

When a hurdler sets into the starting blocks, he envisions himself winning the race before the gun goes off. He imagines his stride effortlessly carrying him over each obstacle that has an opportunity to silence his victory roar and in that moment before his race begins, he has already won in his mind, his heart, and his soul.

As you begin your journey of healing, restoration, and, empowerment I challenge you to envision healing before it begins, feel restored before the pouring of your fibers are complete, and be empowered to keep running towards the finish line of your destiny.

A runner understands that he has a number of hurdles on the track that he must jump over in order to cross the threshold of history, record breaking pandemonium, or tantalizing tactics and you may be on your first, fourth, or ninth hurdle of life. Whatever your obstacle is you have the ability to keep running and win the race.

Your life is about to change forever and I encourage you to buckle up your chinstrap and seatbelt and get your popcorn ready…it is time to revolutionize your destiny and be the man that every woman essentially desires.

PART ONE

HER BEAUTY

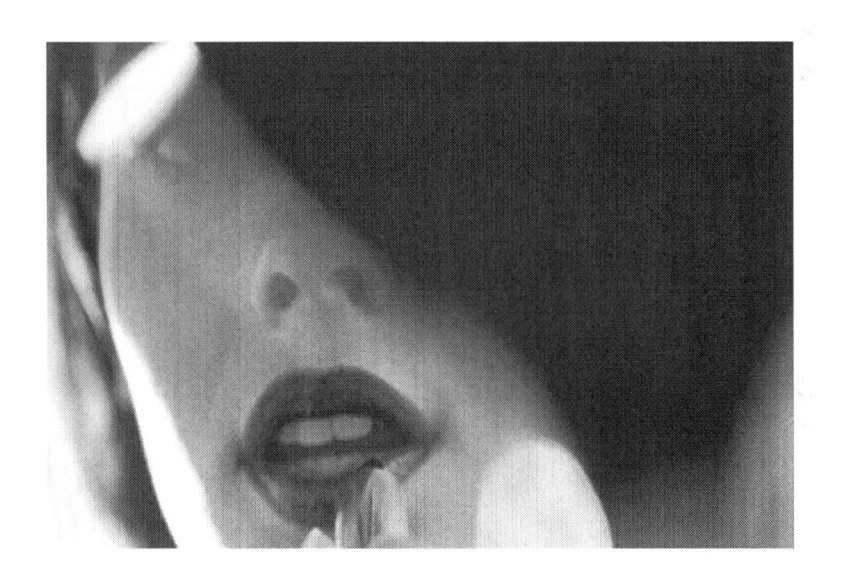

1 WHAT GOT YOU

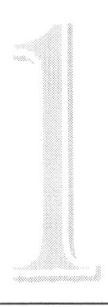

Outward beauty will soon fade but what is stored in the inner chambers of our spirit and heart remains long after gravity has gotten the best of us.

When looking at a brochure for an exotic vacation resort or an advertisement for a new car we are often enticed by what's displayed in the medium not realizing that the marketing director and advertising manager knew exactly what was needed to lure you into the ad and expected the tantalizing graphics, pictures, and catch phrases to entice you to the point that it created what I call a curiosity cushion.

A curiosity cushion allows you to lay in its comfort engaging fantasy while eluding the realities of life. Scientists say the brain functions from linear to holistic, sequential to random, symbolic to concrete, logical to intuitive, verbal to non-verbal and reality-based to fantasy-oriented processing. What criteria does the brain use for distinguishing between real and fiction? Recent research suggests that personal relevance may be a key factor, although there are exceptions. When we are smitten by the beauty of a woman we are like the resort brochure and new car ad I referenced above because it's what she displays that captivates our attention and lures us inward to peek more into her being.

What attracts a man to a woman? Many will argue that the true answer may lie in the original creation of every man because not one of us is the same so the answer will vary. The basic Laws of Attraction suggest, "like attracts like" that positive and negative thinking bring about positive and negative physical results respectively. However, this metaphysical belief is somewhat unwarranted to many who propose that the Law of Attraction may contradict itself. Steve Pavilina, a self-proclaimed personal development coach for "smart people" says the problems are not caused by the Law of Attraction itself but rather by the Law of Attraction as applied to objective reality.

The 2004 movie "Laws of Attraction" starring Pierce Bronson, Julianne Moore and Parker Posey, tells a story of two New York divorce attorneys who are often competing against each other, but end up in a relationship nonetheless. They marry and soon realize that they too will face many of the same issues at home that lead unhappy couples into their place of work. One of the central cases in the story is the heavily publicized divorce of a rock star from his wife. What attracts us to people often times could be the same thing that drives us apart. Bronson and Moore realized that they both were attracted to different things and one attraction was not necessarily the other.

If asked what is the male sex organ, many would respond with the obvious but most men are mostly attracted by what they see, which is why a visually and physically attractive woman tends to appeal to him and capture his attention immediately. All of my adult life and most of my adolescence I often wondered why pretty women tend to draw a bigger crowd at the pool than any other woman. I have since likened those seemingly goddess looking women to a new car on a used car lot. Because of its freshly coated exterior, unscathed seating, low to no mileage and tires with tread thicker than uncut grass in the summer, the new car stands out among all the others on the lot. I am not suggesting that those women who may possess a few flaws or blemishes are unattractive but to the average man she could be viewed as a vehicle with cloth seats versus a leather interior and his preference on this particular day is the shiny new car with leather interior that was just delivered to the car lot.

Contrary to the delectable taste that men possess, the outward beauty of the woman renders her powerful and in fact is one of the characteristics that imprison men and render them helpless to her colorful web of splendor. When I was about eleven years old, my mother took me to downtown Atlanta to ride an exceptional popular ride at one of the oldest retail department stores in the country, Rich's. While in route to what I anticipated as one of the most exciting days of my life I saw a tantalizing, fascinating, awe striking red 1988 Pontiac Fiero. This vehicle had to be one of the most creative and innovative of its time, or so I thought! The way it captivated me and seized my attention spoke highly of its ability to draw potential consumers to its exterior splendor. Most men who are intrigued solely by the beauty of a woman face challenges maneuvering through the relationship because of their failure to *inspect* what they *expect* from that woman. As gorgeous as the Pontiac Fiero was I never inspected anything else about the car before attempting to talk my mother into buying one. Had I done my due diligence I would have found that the vehicle overheated, leaked oil, and while gaining excellent mileage – it was underpowered.

A woman's exterior beauty albeit its fascinating twinkle could conceal a more underlying dilemma once you have had time to unwrap its veneer.

Tip of the Iceberg

Imagine being on a boat and you see a large piece of ice, that has broken off a snow-formed glacier, floating in open water, endangering you and the other passengers. The RMS Titanic met this seemingly innocent piece of ice face to face when it collided with an iceberg while sailing south of the Grand Banks of Newfoundland. The intriguing thing about an Iceberg is that 90% of its mass is beneath the surface. People often times display a portion of who they are to the general public and it is not until they are comfortable with someone that they display their mass. Generally, people show an illusion of who they truly are in the first encounter. I call this façade "Sending the Representative". Think about it, when you meet someone for the first time, whether personal, professional or casual the primary goal is to impress. To accomplish this goal you put your best foot forward. The representative is someone who presents a portion of the person they prefer people to know at that moment in order to gain access before disclosing a more in depth version of who they really are. The representative will be the business partner you've been praying for, the boyfriend or girlfriend you've dreamed about or the friend you've always wanted. Many may wonder what would make a person go through those many phases to deceive, the answer somewhat complex at times but nonetheless logical…they wish to matter, but we will discuss that in a later chapter.

 The tip of the iceberg has its pros and cons, while disclosing your full potential underneath the exterior corridor may be plausible in some aspects it can also be a subtle deception if not properly monitored. Men and women often hide their identity. They are the super hero in disguise, looking to save someone in distress, or a jewel thief eluding detection. The super hero aims to keep a low profile as he strives to perform a beneficial service to the community; therefore, the shielding of his identity is sincere. On the contrary, the jewel thief attempts to deceive, in order to manipulate his victims, so that he can gain access to their valuables – an egocentric act of selfishness.

 When I walked door to door for the innovative advertising agency Adventures in the late 90's one of the key elements to me being successful was not selling. The confused look on your face as you read this is prompting me to simmer in utter laughter because it sounds foolish to be an advertising agent who does not sell. *Right!!!* My manager often said "Everybody loves to buy but no one wants to be sold anything" That simply means we all will go into a shopping center with the intent to buy but are turned off by the salesman who is pushy and somewhat deceptive in his approach to relinquishing his merchandise.

In your quest for companionship, remember you will encounter super-heroes and jewel thieves. At times, you may not be able to discern who is who. Just because you meet a jewel thief in the alley and she steals your heart, only later to pawn it for a shinier toy, doesn't mean that you can't have a similar encounter in the same alley but be rescued by a super-hero who longs to whisk you off into the sunset and save the day. *Can't make others pay for the indescrepancies of those before them.*

Selfish or Stubborn

I often ask men a pivotal question when I am in the position of rendering advice pertaining to a relationship that may be falling apart or bursting out of the seams "Were you Selfish or Stubborn?" Not every man is selfish and stubborn – it could very well be the woman. Regardless of who holds the selfish crown or wears the diamond encrusted stubborn timepiece - either is seemingly likened to the herd of shoppers exiting the grocery store and tripping the alarm. Although its ring is loud and noticeable, neither person acknowledges its chime yet they continue to maneuver to their vehicle as if completely innocent, while the security tag blares from their shopping bag. Many of us will go through relationships, business ventures, or social circles without noticing or conceding that we could be the cause of those relationships going south before the winter.

We see the warning signs but ignore them - red light, yellow light - speed up rather than slowing down

FROM THE HANDS OF DELILAH TO THE ARMS OF SAMSON

I was the blind shopper ignoring the alarm yet continuing to walk out of the store only to get home with the security tag still intact on my purchase. Many are selfish due in part to some sort of neglect suffered either during childhood or as an adolescent. I recall my mother giving me a birthday party when I was about eight years old. I grew up without much; therefore, I cherished this particular party because my mother bought a huge cake with a circus on top along with a table full of gifts. During the party, I noticed a few of my invited guests leaving with items from my table and the ornaments off the cake. I chased them up the corridor frantically yelling, "Give me back my cake". My mental capacity associated the items atop the cake with the entire cake and the traumatic events of that evening scarred me for a very long time. I felt betrayed, angered, and disrespected at the mere notion that someone would take something so special to me. I have since realized that because my mother could not afford to shower me with gifts and material belongings I held closely to the things she provided and the void of not having the latest technology or clothing rendered me very possessive of what I considered my property.

I discovered that the root of my problem did not lie in not having things; it was my anxiety to savor what I had at that moment, perpetuating my selfish nature to consume everything. Many of us are selfish and do not know it! When our selfish behavior boils over, we begin to understand why our stubbornness results in rightly being labeled, a selfish individual.

The dictionary defines stubborn as unreasonably obstinate; obstinately unmoving: fixed or set in purpose or opinion; resolute. I believe when one is present the other is lurking in a dark alley awaiting a signal for arrival. I have heard many men say "This is just the way I am." Although a true statement, in order to build a sustainable relationship, we must be receptive to modifications in our character and personality. As we will learn if we continue growing and growing as we continue learning, we as human beings are unique and possess an internal push button that allows us to adapt to various scenarios, situations, and circumstances. Having this built in mechanism is what allows us to excel in peculiar circumstances and champion life's adversity.

Regardless of our unique individual make up, we must invest in our self-growth as much as we invest into our 401k plans and stock options. Investing in a self-development plan is by far the greatest asset we will ever possess in our relationship-building portfolio.

A selfish man will eventually become a lonely man clamoring to procure love in an empty bowl of stubborn stew laced with an aggravated appetite, detached delicacies and drenched with an enormous side of cupcake compassionless cappuccino.

The Cinderella Effect

Beauty has been defined as an assortment of things over the years. What is considered beautiful to one may not be beautiful to another. I'm sure you have heard the story of Cinderella. You know the beautiful girl with the two mean stepsisters, and wicked stepmother. You already know the ending, the beautiful girl marries the handsome prince and they live happily ever after.

The prince gave chase and persevered in capturing the heart of the woman he viewed as a magnificent jewel. This manifestation of true love intrigued us, the readers.

Unbeknownst to the eager yet uninformed lad, the woman he imagined Cinderella to be was far from the one she actually was. As men, we are naturally drawn to women as flies are drawn to unattended food at the family reunion. Later, we become perplexed to discover that she is not who we envisioned or hoped for her to be. Cinderella, like a number of women, possessed innate beauty - yet it was covered by the hand me downs she was forced to wear due to her unfortunate circumstances. How intriguing that the one who would encourage her heart was a fury feline she spent long hours all alone with when her wicked stepmother and stepsisters allowed her to rest.

The cat often reminded Cinderella that with all of their expensive clothing garments, jewelry and, stylish vehicles neither of her stepsisters encompassed what she did…BEAUTY! Cinderella, even dressed in old rags was a lovely girl. Her stepsisters, no matter how splendid and elegant their clothes, remained clumsy, lumpy and ugly. As horrid as Cinderella was treated, it was that one moment in time that changed her life forever. It only takes one Moment.

How many of us wish we had a fairy godmother who could transform us from our miry, gloomy selves into the Knight we desire to be – all with the flick of a magic wand. The beauty I want you to understand is not the physical one from this story but the one you hold on the inside. Cinderella felt like many of us attempting to stand out in a crowded room or compete for a position at work. You may not be beautiful like Cinderella who was mistreated by her stepmother and stepsisters; and, you may not be looking to be noticed by a princess at a ball. However, you may be the fury feline who can uplift and encourage people during their intimate time of need. You may be the one who can help women finally become aware of why everyone continues to stare when they walk into the room.

I am coming to terms with the fact that, in this journey entitled "LIFE", we will encounter a number of women who will hold undeniable beauty. Although we are tempted to engage merely for that verity, it is only surface and will require us to inspect further so that our expectations are not always depleted leaving us frustrated with beauty. While our sexual organ views beauty as an attractive signal, for a number of men, beauty is what we find at the dig site when searching for that missing treasure - that treasure that captures the heart beyond the physical. You will learn a great deal if you continue living, but most importantly, as you venture strive to be more of the solution versus a propagating problem.

Bread Heels

It has always intrigued me as to why so many will sift through an entire loaf of bread to avoid the seemingly dreadful heel atop and then leave the bread to mold. People often say that heels are rich in nutrients. Many of us have, at some point, felt like or been seen as the ghastly bread heel in our lives, overlooked for what appears to be a more enriching slice of bread. I have learned that we must discover our own worth and not look to validate it through what others say or feel about us. As painful as it is to want to feel accepted, we must understand that we were created with value and the priceless ornaments of beauty we will find along our journey cannot be defined by how we look, what we drive, where we live, or how much social or financial status we may obtain in life.

Bread heels are often ignored or wasted because of their appearance. What you see is not always, what you will get and the perceived is not always the perception. You must learn the value of your being. Understand the beauty you already possess. Learn how to empower others to discover their true beauty.

THE CURVES OF SOCIAL MEDIA

Life may throw a curve ball so illusive that it seems difficult to hit it and begins the question of if the illusions even exist.

Social media has exploded in cyber space over the past few years connecting audiences across the globe with the latest news, providing exciting entertainment, music, video, and reuniting childhood friends and classmates. One of the most eluding things about Social Media is everyone can become someone with a few clicks of a button. Social Media outlets can be very eluding when it comes to identifying the true characteristics of a person. People often hide who they really are behind artificial avatar pictures and overtly inflated profile descriptions. Everyone is beautiful online because it allows us to escape the realities of whatever life we may have and enter into a fantasy vault that enables us to become Academy Award winning actors.

The irony of the internet being a viable source of information is although it is helpful in one area it can be very critical in another. I recall a woman requesting my friendship on Facebook and because I am one of the few who doesn't have to know you personally to accept your online friendship accepted her with no investigation. My acceptance I must admit was due in part because her profile picture looked very familiar as if I either knew her personally or had met her at an event at some point. This woman portrayed the perfect wife, mother and sister. She had the perfect family it seemed having left a lucrative position at a prestigious law firm in New York City to relocate to Atlanta to assist her husband in expanding his thriving business was very commendable I thought. Soon after she settled in her new city, she was whisking in and out of bridal stores with her daughter preparing for her big day of nuptials while searching for her new venture in "Hotlanta".

I found her love for her family quite evocative and inviting, she often spoke of her entire family when we interacted. Her sister was a high school principal, her mother a decorated police officer, one of her sisters was a successful model, the other a happily married mom of two whose husband was a pro athlete and her other daughter was attending Harvard while her son was a model in California. I thought this was the next thing to the popular TV family on the 80's hit show "The Cosby Show". Surely, Cliff and Clair were just a click away along with Rudy, Olivia, Vanessa, Denise, Sonya, and Theo behind the Facebook template awaiting the curtain call to unveil them. This ordeal seemed too good to be true and honestly began to concern me. The first thing I observed about this family was everyone had a professional looking profile picture. That was not my sole issue but *ALL* of their pictures were professional and perfect. I figured at some point no matter who you are or what you do you will at one moment or another upload a picture of you, your friends or family at an outing of some sort but nothing with this family they seemed to perfect. One day Vanessa, my mystery social media friend said to me that she had purchased one of my empowering apparel shirts and even uploaded a graphic as her profile picture. This abrupt action raised caution and caused the radar in my inner bull crap reader to explode primarily because we receive precise reports on purchases and had not been notified of any new purchases that day or the one before so I wondered why the blatant lie. The next morning Vanessa was up and at it early, as I logged on to my Facebook account a lengthy message awaited. In her caring and charismatic demeanor, she inquired about my morning and proceeded to share her night and vibrantly expecting day. Vanessa's actions the day before disturbed me so much that I stayed up all night investigating this mystery woman and her seemingly perfect family.

As a kid, I always wanted to work for the FBI or Secret Service so was very fond of investigative reporting and crime dramas on television. I knew my Law & Order, CSI, and Brenda Lee Johnson the Closer tactics would come in handy and I was certain this was the perfect scenario to utilize my television degree to highlight my investigative techniques and crime solving skills without truly knowing if a crime had indeed been committed. The more digging I did the more I began to uncover. First, Vanessa's profile picture as my initial instincts suspected was a fraud. It appeared the woman in the picture was familiar to me because she was a well-known actor I'd seen on television. My discovery unveiled that one of her sisters profile picture was a hair model's photograph who was displayed in a well-known magazine. If that was not enough of a fairytale, her mother's picture was that of a retired police officer in a huge metropolitan city. My eyes lit up when I saw the message from Vanessa because here was my chance to reel in what I had discovered to be a very fraudulent account and report the fake Vanessa to the authorities. I gave Vanessa an opportunity to tell me the truth by asking a few opulent questions like "Are you sure that's you in your profile picture", she replied "of course who else would it be". I then informed her that it was very strange because her profile picture was exactly the one my friend had of his girlfriend over the fireplace in his home in which I was presently visiting. The internet airwaves went silent as Vanessa rendered no response for about five minutes and then something unseemly happened...Vanessa deleted her account, her sisters, all of her children, and when I informed her that I knew about her son, and her mother's page she followed with their deletion as well.

Hollow-Man

What an experience that roller coaster was and I realized that my instincts were indeed correct, that family was too good to be true. To imagine someone creating multiple lives of fairytale fantasy on a social networking site was perplexing and disturbing. I could not fathom why someone would go to those lengths to pretend to be multiple people. Was this someone with a schizophrenic personality or someone crying silently for attention?

I was reminded of the 2000 movie Hollow Man. Sebastian Caine is a brilliant yet arrogant scientist working on a top-secret mission for the U.S. government -- to unlock the secret to human invisibility. After creating a serum that induces invisibility in laboratory animals, he disobeys Pentagon orders by trying the serum on himself. Though it works, the effects are irreversible. While his chief lieutenants Linda McKay and Matt Kensington try frantically to counteract the effect, Caine becomes increasingly intoxicated by his newfound power. Not only do his latent megalomaniac tendencies begin to emerge, they get stronger the longer he remains invisible as he begins to perceive all efforts to cure him as a threat to his very existence.

Many become so engrossed in being someone of imagination that the illusions of becoming the dream overshadow the reality of living by original design. Vanessa, who could have been a 10 year old boy, a 35 year old man or a 21 year old college girl, became like Sebastian Caine engrossed in the deceitful lies of her profile image that she lost touch or interest in living her true identity. Vanessa went to great lengths to create an entire fable family to conceal the authentic rationale of her seemingly unhappy truth.

Many of us who have experienced some type of hurt or let down have become hollow and won't allow others to see who we truly are for fear that who we are isn't enough. You are worth more than you know and although at times, you may not feel very worthy of any type of affection, adoration, or love, Jesus paid a price for you and you paid a price through your life experiences for your anointing I strongly suggest that you sell it not.! NOT FOR SALE!

Allowing your Hollow Man to supersede you will inadvertently disable your unique being and force others to be subjected to a pseudo you versus an authentic you.

Swing for the Fence

In the game of baseball, players can often be heard throughout the clubhouse as saying "Swing For the Fence". This phrase means that once at bat give it everything you have and when the pitch is thrown no matter what type it is, to swing with the intent of hitting the ball over the fence therefore, hitting a homerun. Only twenty-seven instances in the history of Major League baseball have actually accomplished that feat. Fourteen are in the American League, thirteen are in the National League, eight of the home runs hit with the first pitch ever were done by pitchers, and two were grand slams! Many men and women are swinging for the fence on the first pitch meaning they are looking at second base before landing on first. Anything that is made well is made slow...You must be patient with the process. Don't allow your anxiety to date throw you into a social media frenzy swinging at any pitch thrown by your cyber fantasy attempting to knock it out of the park before you get the proper signal from your batting coach. Athletes practice so that they may improve because they understand that at any given moment they could operate in enough perfection to win the game. You will win in life by carefully monitoring how you approach the game of dating and relationship. Be empowered beyond empowerment, live to change…change to live!

3 FISHING FOR FOOL'S GOLD

In the pond of life lie a great deal of exotic jewels, be very careful of the catch and pay attention to details, for with wisdom comes a thirst for understanding and with understanding comes a responsibility and that responsibility is the key to obtaining true treasures.

We have often heard the term seek and you will find, yet I believe it's what we are in search of that is the key ingredient to what we find being valuable or fool's gold. Many of us are programmed as young men that having a stable of beautiful women was some sort of rite of passage to manhood. It is that type of thinking that has garnered men incapable of staying committed to or engrossed in meaningful relationships. The options may be vast but the qualities of choices are few.

What is fool's gold? Fool's gold also known as iron pyrite is a gold-colored mineral that is often mistaken for real gold. Fool's gold is also a common term used to describe any item which has been believed to be valuable to the owner, only to end up being not so. Those investments in hot stocks that seemed too good to be true, only to crash and burn, can be referred to as investing in fool's gold. During historical periods of gold rushes, many less-than-knowledgeable miners would frequently believe that they hit the mother lode upon finding a cache of fool's gold. Unfortunately, unlike the real thing, fool's gold is relatively worthless.

We often see the caramel brown skin, the sensual curves and voluptuous demeanor of a woman's exterior without inspecting what we expect and find ourselves attracted to her sparkle and shine but like fool's gold, find out that beyond her looks she is nothing close to being the real gold we were after.

I remember my mother gave me a watch and because of my fondness of this exquisite timepiece, I did not bother to research its value yet I merely saw it as an object to keep time. I stored the watch in my gym bag while playing basketball only to find it gone when I returned to retrieve it. I later would discover that the item cost a staggering $1300. Because I never knew the value the item I possessed held, I was not able to care for it properly nor was I able to protect it from vultures who knew its value. Many of us never take the time to observe the treasures that we may possess because we either devalue them or consider those jewels replaceable. I was never able to replace my stolen watch and found it difficult to deal with the ramifications that I would face. The lesson I learned haunted me for quite some time and to this day often lingers in the back of my mind.

Relationships can be golden nuggets of inspiration if chosen correctly or faltering frustrations of chaos if not. A fisherman is a person who fishes, whether for profit or pleasure, what you must ask yourself is what are you fishing for and is it to gain some sort of profit or is it for personal pleasure?

We will often find things in our search that we can neither use nor desire. I urge you to examine the essentials. The things that may have once been a priority to you at one point may not be the same today. Therefore, your quest for finding a mate who will be able to substantiate your needs at the present may not possess the superficial qualities you craved before and may hold a more long-standing quality that could be overlooked due to impaired vision.

As you continue in your search of a compatible mate, study the rules and regulations to fishing. The rules may vary from state to state and mate to mate. You will need the following to maneuver through various obstacles or hindrances that may prohibit you from finding the real jewels versus fool's gold:

Fish in Public Fishing Areas- Fishing in your neighbor's pond is illegal and trespassers may be subject to arrest and penalty by law. (Read between the lines here)

Recreational Fishing is not Recommended- Relinquish the myth that shopping without a purpose is the rite of passage to becoming a man. A man who searches with no goal in mind is wandering aimlessly and will never find the end of his journey.

Understand the Various Types of Fish in the Lake- You must understand that every woman is not the same and will not have identical objectives, goals, or attractions. Take time to learn her needs and discover your own, so that you may be an asset to her and her to you.

DADDY CREATED THIS 4

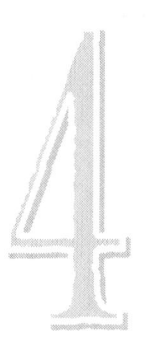

My children, listen when your father corrects you. Pay attention and learn good judgment, for I am giving you good guidance. Don't turn away from my instructions. For I, too, was once my father's son, tenderly loved as my mother's only child. Proverbs 4:1-3

Imagine cupping in your hands a pile of clay and rolling it around in your hands until it formed the splendid design you desired. Many of us are who we are today because of how our fathers shaped us. Regardless if your father was in the home or your life for the most part, a great deal of what he did or did not do has assisted in shaping the man you are at this moment. I have a fond memory of my father who as a child was not as involved as much as I would have wanted but an enjoyable evening at the movies helped me retain memories of our connection and endless moments together. A miscommunication between him and my mother caused my father to disappear into the musky air of the night like a ghost when I was around eleven years old. I would learn some twenty-five years later that he regretted the decision to both leave and stay gone for so long.

We develop characteristics of our parents be it good, bad or indifferent that often shape who we will become. I struggled most of my life with commitment and could not understand why it was so difficult to sustain a monogamous relationship. As a child and up until my late teens I had very few memories of my father and the ones I did have I locked up in my emotional vault very tightly. We never had the talk about the "Birds and the Bees". My mother who did an extraordinary job raising me and my two brothers, was an all purpose person who attempted like most single moms to be both mother and father but it just wasn't practical for her to do so.

She never really had the "TALK" with me but did attempt a subtle version when I was in my twenties. I thought, "I'm too old for this now!" she didn't go hardcore with me she was very timid as if to say although it was necessary, she wasn't fully equipped or prepared to have the sex or relationship talk with her now grown son. My father up until 2003 wasn't present much so I knew very little about his relationship DNA and therefore a number of my inherited traits often left me bewildered or unaware of their originated source.

My father came to visit me in the spring of 2011 and we enjoyed each other's company for about thirty days or so and in that time we were able to hash out a few things as well as, learn a great deal about one another. It was in this time that I began to notice a few habits that seemed familiar and more so a few characteristics and traits that resembled my behavior. I won't address a number of those discoveries out of respect of my father's privacy but, will share that his charismatic gift to ignite a conversation with people was alarming but, it was his ability to disarm women that prompted me to take notice. I realized that my poetic gift to comfort, engage, educate, and empower people was a direct relation to the genes I had inherited from my father. I would listen to his genuine concern for total strangers and his ability to defuse any hostile situation with a calm tone and a humble demeanor. I felt as if I had met this person before, referring to my father's character and in turn say that I saw a mirror of myself in my father.

We will often portray characteristics of our parents without knowledge. Sometimes that is a good thing and other times it is not. I learned that my father was never married to my mother but was married before and although I am not sure what caused the rift in that relationship, he has never married again. A huge part of me believes that my father experienced what many men have during his marriage and, that somehow damaged him to a degree that he has never felt compelled to marry again. I say that because in talking with my father and observing him, I often get the sense that he is searching for something, attempting to fill a void or hole in his emotional heart and has been unsuccessful in his attempts.

I also believe that my father and a host of men like him find it difficult to fill those plugs in their heart valves of love because of several reasons including the following:

- **Proper Identification Required**: We cannot honestly correct problems if we have not properly identified **a.)** The cause **b.)** Serum needed to restore **c.)** Recuperation time necessary to restore and replenish.

- **Truth Vaccination**: The truth often causes fear to suffocate what we know and replace it with what we think. A good shot of honesty in the booty would help us be realistic with our expectations.

Finding Fish

We can sometimes search our entire lifetime for something that unknowingly we have not identified. At times, it may take someone else showing us how to locate it so that we are more productive in living out our purpose. Author, director and screenwriter Antwone Fisher wrote a remarkable book entitled *"Finding Fish"* which is an autobiographical account of his life.

In 2002, the American drama film *Antwone Fisher* based upon Fisher's book and directed by Denzel Washington, marking his directorial debut was released. Washington also stars in the film as the psychiatrist Jerome Davenport, alongside Hollywood actor Derek Luke, who plays the title role (and personally knew the real Antwone Fisher), and ex-model Joy Bryant, as Fisher's girlfriend. The movie focuses on Antwone "Fish" Fisher (Derek Luke), a temperamental young man in the navy with a violent history. His father was killed before he was born and his teenage mother, Eva Mae Fisher, was arrested soon after and put in jail where she gave birth to him. He was then placed in an orphanage until she got out to claim him. When she never claimed him, Antwone was placed in a foster home at two years old ran by a religious couple Mr. and Mrs. Tate (Ellis Williams and Novella Nelson). There, Antwone faced abuse by Mrs. Tate both mentally and physically for many years until he finally left the home at age sixteen. Living out on the streets for the next few years, he decided to join the U.S. Navy to make something out of his life. However, the rough life he had as child caused him to have a violent temper at this point.

Fish, spent a majority of his life searching for the love and acceptance he lacked from his mother and healing he needed from the abuse he suffered throughout his early childhood. How many of you are in search of the missing pieces that seem to elude you and may have contributed to a number of life choices that you have made? In the end, Fish found what he needed and that was family and a clear understanding of himself through the help of the doctor. You may not have a professional doctor working with you to draw out those emotional roadblocks but you are not confined by the forest of your past and, will not be defined by the scars of your predicaments yet, you can be empowered to take control of your present and win the war because losing is simply not an option.

Leaving A Scar

After my car accident in 1995, I required a few surgeries that left me both in pain and with a lasting scar. The impact of the accident caused an injury and the injury-required repair in order for healing to commence. During the healing process, a residue of reminder was left by the healed wound primarily known as a scar.

A scar is a mark, a lasting aftereffect, a blemish that is a result of or from suffering some sort of trauma and, undoubtedly is a mark that indicates a former point of attachment. A few things rang out in my mind as I mentioned the above; many of us have encountered an emotional injury as I suspect my father did in his marriage and that injury-required surgery. Instead of allowing a licensed physician to perform the procedure, many of us tend to self medicate and operate! Pain can be unbearable at times and our natural tolerance is not high enough to withstand its penetrating effects. A lingering pain caused by disappointment, rejection, or sudden trauma often leaves us aimlessly wondering in the land of "What If's" constantly questioning what we could have done to prevent the excruciating feeling in our broken hearts that we feel now.

Cocoa Butter Heals All Wounds

When I was, around ten years old I was very fascinated with pro wrestling and eager to try all of the moves I saw on television. One day I decided that I was going to demonstrate my prowess on one of my friends in my neighborhood and orchestrated a makeshift wrestling ring out of his front porch, which hoisted banisters and an entrance made of solid steel. We began playfully running around the ring hitting, slapping, and trash talking just like the people on television. He then pretended to throw me out of the ring onto the arena floor so that we may appease the gathering crowd and make our fantasy to be real life wrestlers come true. As he approached me to ignite his move, I countered with a throat tap, followed by a neck hook and then proceeded to do what they called a DDT (Death Dropping Tackle) move that caused me to snap his neck while smashing his face in the ground. (I know this sounds very gruesome but we had the pretend part down to a science so we weren't suppose to really get hurt) and I say really because after all it was pretend. But something went horribly wrong during our exhibition and as I went to the grown with what was supposed to be my final move he slipped the headlock and threw me backwards and there was a snap, crackle, and then a pop! I looked through the gaping hole in my pants and saw red, white and blue and I am not talking about the American flag either. It seemed that my leg was severely cut open because I had fallen on broken glass; I was rushed to the hospital and sixty-four stitches and staples were inserted to put my leg back together.

The incident left me out of school for a few weeks. The huge scar the injury left was awe striking and the doctors advised my mother to put Cocoa Butter on the wound as it healed to alleviate cracking and, to smooth the marks left from the injury. I never understood how I could put cocoa butter on my injury everyday sometimes more than once but could still view the injury. Today, I can still see the injury because it never actually went away but what the cocoa butter did was assist with the healing of the scar and although I could visibly see, the after affects of the injury, I no longer felt the pained it caused. What we must learn to do with pain is soothe the injury with Cocoa Butter and although we may visibly see the affects of that hurt, it will no longer affect us as it did when initiated.

The following are some techniques you can use to heal the scars left by past hurt:

Exercise:
- Train your mind to think positively
- Grow as you learn from mistakes or choices and learn as you begin to grow in life.

Meditate:
- Reflect on the wins…if you focus on the loses in life it will affect your ability to win any more races.
- Renew your mind-overhaul your thinking versus overloading it with the "Why's" of life.

Read:
- Increase your intellectual power and ability with faith-filled thoughts.
- What you put in your mind determines what comes out in your words or actions.
- What you feed your mind is just as important as what you feed your body. Monitor your intake.

Overall healing is a process and you must be committed to the marathon of healing versus the sprint of bitterness. Yesterday's wounds will eventually become tomorrow's stories of triumph if you desire to mend the broken pieces and allow yourself adequate time to heal.

5 BROKE, SICK AND LONELY

A man lacking money isn't broke yet poor by definition, A man who is ill isn't sick but lacks the mobility to gain health, A man who is alone isn't lonely yet he sits in silence awaiting instructions for his journey. —Mo Stegall

I believe when we allow our greed to drive us versus the whisper of character or integrity, we are subjecting ourselves to a clear path of destruction that will leave us broke, sick and lonely. I read a story of a man who amassed a great deal of wealth by assumingly deceiving innocent people and stealing their money. The man, a native Texan who was knighted by the government of Antigua in 2006, is accused of misleading investors about certificates of deposit (CDs) issued by his offshore bank, in one of the biggest white-collar fraud cases since Bernard Madoff.

The CDs were touted as safe, with funds "generally invested in investment grade bonds, securities and foreign currency deposit," according to literature distributed by his brokerage firm.

Instead, prosecutors allege, he invested CD proceeds in illiquid pet-project investments that included Caribbean real estate, a Cowboys and Indians magazine and a pawnshop operator. He also loaned more than $2 billion to himself.

The alleged Ponzi scheme started to unravel in late 2008 as the financial crisis deepened and more and more investors asked for redemptions, a situation that left Stanford scrambling for cash. He is also said to have falsified financial statements and made false statements about his bank's financial condition.

"No one is exempt or off limits when it comes to the **TRUTH!** *We must discontinue our quest to make mortal men God's of immortality!"* –*Mo Stegall*

His health has declined since his arrest. He was injured in a jailhouse brawl in 2009 and suffered from an addiction to a powerful anti-anxiety medication. He has hepatitis B and cirrhosis of the liver, and, if convicted, will likely spend the rest of his life in prison.

The SEC seized all of his assets in February 2009 after filing a civil lawsuit. His lawyer at the time, Dick DeGuerin, said the government's action did not even leave enough money for his client to buy underwear.

Once No. 205 on Forbes' list of richest Americans, his defense is paid for with U.S. tax dollars and his 81-year-old mother is struggling to help.

"I've maxed out my credit cards and I'm on my last few thousand dollars of savings," said the mother.

After his arrest, the embattled man had a bevy of women, four of whom are mothers of his six children, attend his court hearings. He had a "fiancée" half his age even though he remains legally married. He lavished the women in his life with trips on private jets, luxury homes and, in one instance, spousal support payments of $100,000 per month, according to court documents.

His oldest daughter, Randi, lived in a luxury Houston high-rise paid for by her father, for whom she worked.

Court records from a 2007 paternity case, that was settled, showed he also paid about $150,000 a year in child support for two other children who lived with their mother in a $10 million house in Florida.

Now, in addition to losing his fortune, he has only the support of his parents and family and not the harem of loyalists seen earlier.

Only his mother lasted through the entire three days of testimony at a hearing in which he was judged competent to stand trial.

The man who once ran a business with operations in 140 countries has different priorities now. In a recent court hearing, he could be heard complaining about being served a peanut butter sandwich on stale bread.

The road to a successful you or a successful personal or professional relationship will begin with you opting to build those on integrity filled, character driven modules that allow you to discern deceit, manipulation and corruption yet allowing your heart to be absorbed with love, compassion and honesty. Many have come before with a more complex formula and have failed miserably; you have a choice of how you will live and how you will be remembered.

The man in the story will more than likely spend the rest of his fragile life regretting those decisions that he no longer have the power to change yet can change how he views his progression moving forward. He may never reclaim the glory of those moments spent flying across the country on private jets or spending thousands on tailored suits but he can leave a legacy of who he became after the fall versus who he was during it.

If you invest frivolously in relationships that are unproductive or exploitive, you may find yourself a repeat contestant on the Broke, Sick, and Lonely game show.

PART ONE: HER BEAUTY

⏻ Power Point to Ponder

Appearance is important to us, and we spend time and billions of dollars a year improving it, but how much effort do we put into developing our inner beauty? Tolerance, compassion and joyfulness are the beauty treatments that assist us in becoming truly lovely on the inside. In order for you to value the beauty of someone else, you must discover that of your own.

❓ Question to Consider

In your quest to find a mate, have you only sought the outer beauty, physical appearance, superficial qualities? Have you suffered from a lack of intimacy from your parents? or Because of bad investments are you feeling broke, sick and lonely?

◇ Jewel Tip

In your quest for love, do not smother your potential with your expectations.

POWER NOTES:

PART TWO

HER VOICE

HONEY LIPS 6

For the lips of an immoral woman are as sweet as honey, and her mouth is smoother than oil. But in the end she is as bitter as poison, as dangerous as a double-edged sword. Her feet go down to death; her steps lead straight to the grave. For she cares nothing about the path to life. She staggers down a crooked trail and doesn't realize it.
Proverbs 5:3-6

The bible says that any person should be on guard against those who use flattery and smooth talk (lips that are sweet as honey) that would lead him or her into sin. The best advice is to take a detour and even avoid conversation with such people. The immoral woman that the above scripture is speaking of is a prostitute. Now for many of you reading you are saying "I've never had an encounter with or been solicited by a prostitute", maybe not physically but many of us have been manipulated vocally by someone with illicit motives. Many affairs and fantasies began with either visual presentations or devious conversations disguised as common chatter.

I have always admired the taste of honey in my tea or on my Honey Nut Cheerios and its distinctive taste savors in my mouth and prompts me to want more and more of it. An attraction does not care whom it caters toward, its primary objective is to draw you closer to it. When I met, my wife she had lips that I thought screamed they needed some attention. Many of you have either said the same about someone or felt that way yourself about your own lips, regardless there is something extraordinarily sexy in my option about lips that are appealing and inviting nonetheless, the opposite to lips that are crusty followed by kisses that are sloppy and oversaturated with saliva.

   The right combination of sultry sex appeal and opulent vocal manipulation can render anyone helpless to the deadly poison of a honey lip driven conversation. Many men have engage in conversations and many have initiated those same conversations, some oblivious to its content while others fully aware of the deceit of their intent. Matters not which side of the spectrum you may have landed it is important that you begin to take inventory of the conversations you initiate and entertain for the long lasting echoes of its affect may prove to be costly.

The Poison In Her Voice Will Paralyze You

Have you ever been bitten by anything poisonous? Aside from a bee sting as a child, I have never been bitten or stung by an insect or animal as most of you reading this book probably have that same testimony yet the pain of love and relationship has bitten me several times. Research shows that in all of the relationships that may have ended painfully that none compare to being bitten by a poisonous insect or animal with venom that includes paralysis. The Sea Wasp also known as the Box Jellyfish all glowing and undulating, pulsating with unearthly beauty is the world's most deadly jelly fish and each one packs enough venom to kill 60 adults. They have tentacles up to 3 meters long and just brushing one is enough to automatically release the microscopic darts flooding your system with poison.

Excruciating pain follows shortly, and if the strike is bad, your expected lifespan is somewhere around 3 or 4 minutes.

There is nothing subtle, sweet or sultry about the venom of a woman's paralyzing voice. As Delilah demonstrated her voice had a significant effect on Samson's methods of operation, she understood the power her persistence held and her manipulative motives drove her to fully exhaust herself into wearing him down in order to conqueror the secrets of his strength. Men across the globe have engaged in dangerous dialogue unbeknownst to the jeopardy they were putting themselves in and never realizing that the power shifted when they revealed their secrets.

You may ask what drives a man to relinquish his ability to decipher exploitation from exuberant intent or deceitful dialogue from delightful discussion; many are smitten by an illusion of undefined love or enthralled by the plethora of beautiful booty present on the smorgasbords of corporate offices, campus classrooms, church pews, and community canvases.

I recall when I was around twelve years old, my brother Shawn, childhood friend Daryl and I were playing at home while my mother was at work. While on the porch our neighbors who were a clad of young and vivacious majesty women, possessing beauty like a ancient century goddess and bodies of well sculpted statues on display at a national museum engaged us in a conversation that led to a robbery.

Ok I will not leave you in suspense, the young women who ranged in age between 17yrs-24yrsold needed a few items to cook lunch for themselves and their children and asked if they could borrow something from our pantry. My mother was a stickler on not allowing things to leave the house without her permission and because my butt was not in the mood to have a private meeting with her belt, I withdrew my petition to disobey my mother's wishes. The women were very persistent much like that of Delilah and began to spew sexual rhetoric to a couple of horny teenagers that most likely wanted to hear it and for the most part it worked.

They instructed us to leave the door unlocked and go up stairs and get naked but not to peep. They would ensue to give us an experience we would never forget. Unfortunately, for them my twelve-year-old mind was operating as if it was already twenty-four and something about their sudden generosity did not sit well with me and I proceeded to hide behind the sofa downstairs before they arrived. I heard chatter and whispers and grew more excited because I could not believe that I was mere minutes away from losing my virginity to what I considered a group of classy and seasoned women. The instincts that we possess will often alert us to when something is not right and urges us when we need to remove ourselves from a situation is a great asset and we should pay close attention to it. At twelve-years-old, I was not able to determine what that was and therefore upon hearing the chatter, I emerged from behind the sofa prematurely and missed an opportunity to save myself, my brother and Daryl from what lied ahead.

They make their tongues as sharp as a serpent's; the poison of vipers is on their lips-Psalm 140:3

What's Heard...What's Said

When I jumped from behind the sofa and exposed my hiding place; the women were frantic and begin to alter what I saw into what they said. Maybe that sounds a bit confusing so let me explain, I overheard the women plotting to steal food from my mother's pantry and that's what caused me to emerge from behind the sofa but because we were a few excited teens with enormous hormones the young women used that to their advantage. By revealing myself prematurely it caused me not to catch them in their deceitful plan and granted me a one-way ticket to exotic prison as they ushered me upstairs with a beautiful escort who would make sure we did not reemerge from the upstairs bedroom before they had completely wiped us out of everything we had in the pantry.

We heard one thing but another was being said and because of our inattentive ears, we only heard what we wanted. The women devised a manipulative plan from the beginning and utilize our youthful minds to manipulate us. They coerced us into giving them what they wanted without giving us anything in return. Many of us are given the warning signs early on some even at the point of reference when we meet people who say one thing but mean another. What is heard and what is said are the same but interpreted differently. We will often program ourselves to hear the things we desire because we have hope that we will get what we want yet when the writing is on the wall we tend to ignore the obvious to fulfill a fantasy that unfortunately will never materialize.

My initial feelings about those women were right on point and because my immature mind could not digest the information exponentially and because of the feelings associated I could not make the proper decision necessary to save myself from further damage caused by the manipulative women.

That incident caused me to unknowingly grow a disdain disliking to certain types of women whom I deemed pretty, sexy, and sexually attractive. Many of you reading this book may ask why did that incident seemingly scar me for a very long time, I will attempt to paint the picture a bit clearer for you. After my escort upstairs, I hid again in a closet and watched the escort leave once my brother and friend were completely naked. Her tone and conversation wreaked of more disgusting promises that she knew would never come to fruition, she ran down the steps and I followed shortly thereafter only to find the door fastened and no naked women lounging on the living room sofa. I did not immediately see anything out of order but a knock on the door from a neighbor gave me the impression that it was not all good in Mr. Rogers's neighborhood. He handed me a small bag with a few groceries and instructed me to put them back before my mother came home. I stood at the door utterly confused and bewildered. How could women so beautiful deceive so hard? Why would someone who seemingly cared for us steal from us? So many questions plagued my mind at that moment but, I also felt relieved to escape a bullet with them taking the food because I thought they returned everything that they stole...**WRONG!!!**

We would quickly find out the hard truth about the mystery women who coerced a few boys into feeding their families on a fraudulent promise of promiscuity. When my mother arrived home and began preparing dinner, she immediately noticed all of the missing items. *(After all this is the woman who bought the groceries and prepared the meals daily, so of course she would notice anything out of place).* She summoned us to the kitchen and asked what happened to all of our food. My immediate thoughts were the women who were chattering in the kitchen earlier in the day when we thought we were about to become made men, as if our last names were Gambino or Capone. Once we revealed to my mother that the neighbors paid us a visit, the windows of heaven were open but a blessing was not poured out. Because of our choice, we received a stiff punishment along with an embarrassing and painful spanking. My mother had an altercation with the women next door and it was awful. That day left me feeling violated and confused about women and their intentions when it related to relationships. It caused me to have a subtle distrust for the women I would meet later in my life.

I have learned that we have two ears and one mouth so we should be found listening more than we are speaking but pay closer attention to what others are not saying. People tend to speak what is in their heart according to scripture found in ***Luke 6:45*** *A good man out of the good treasure of his heart bringeth forth that which is good; and an evil man out of the evil treasure of his heart bringeth forth that which is evil: for of the* *abundance of the heart his mouth speaketh.* Be sure that you are listening for the matters of the heart.

7 LYING TO LIVE: DECEPTICONS

The wicked earneth deceitful wages; but he that soweth righteousness hath a sure reward. Proverbs 11:18

It's rather fascinating to envision an automobile being able to speak yet today we have vehicles that tell us the date, time and the weather forecast. It may be even more far fetching to picture an automobile being able to transform from riding to walking. Several decades ago Japanese toy company Takara, which was eventually bought by American company Hasbro, thought that idea was interesting and therefore created the now popular Transformers, robots that transform to vehicles and help humans fight crime and destruction on earth. The Transformers hailed from the fictional universe Cybertron that had its share of power struggles and its ongoing battle between good and evil. The Autobots most notably known as the protagonist find themselves always in an upheaval clash with the antagonists' villains known as The Decepticons.

The villains take many forms, and have many different origins and stories across the numerous different Transformers media, but in almost all incarnations, Megatron leads them. They are typically

represented by the purple facial insignia they all wear. Primarily, Decepticons have red eyes, while Autobots have blue eyes. They are usually known for their air power, especially since many of them transform into aircrafts. They often transform into military vehicles, construction vehicles, and even smaller-than-human-sized objects.

The Decepticons are a malevolent race of robot warriors, brutal and merciless. The Decepticons are driven by a single undeviating goal: total domination of the universe. In the war that raged between the Decepticons and Autobots for millions of years, their home planet of Cybertron was drained of its once rich sources of energy. In hopes of finding new reserves for making Energon, their basic fuel, the Decepticons followed the Autobots to Earth. Under the leadership of the ruthless Megatron, they continued their efforts to destroy the remaining Autobot forces. They attacked throughout the Earth and in space, using their underwater Decepticon headquarters as their staging base and bunker.

In our encounters of life we have either met or more than likely will meet many Decepticons, who are disguised as one thing but, in actuality are something entirely different. As with the fictional characters in the popular series, the Decepticons you will meet have a mission. The mission is to separate you from your heart and emotions, voiding you of any real feelings of intimacy, love or sincere care. I met a young man in Seattle, WA name Anthony Grier while traveling as the Youth Empowerment Ambassador for the National Urban League who shared with me his encounter with a Decepticon better known as his ex-wife. I use the term not to be endearing or disrespectful to her. He met her while working in his company's satellite office and had an instant connection but the steamy fairytale dream soon turned into a nightmare six months after they were married. Their eyes met in the lobby while he was in route to a business meeting and he immediately felt compelled to stop and ask her name however, he was whisked into the elevator and hauled off to a stuffy office across town. Throughout the day his body was in the intense financial meeting yet his mind, spirit and, soul were back at his corporate office on Yasmin, the woman he stole a glimpse of a few hours prior. He hurried back to the office hoping that she was still lingering in the lobby. He made it just in time. She was leaving. After her day of observation, she decided that the company did not meet her career goals and was on her way home when Anthony approached her. He fumbled around a few ice-breaking questions; apparently, Yasmin had her eyes on him as well and made the awkward transition a bit smoother. The two of them hit it off at once and seemed inseparable with Yasmin often joining Anthony at company gatherings. They were married shortly thereafter and so the journey commenced.

Transformers: Exodus and Exile

Anthony was a loving, caring, unselfish mama's boy who loved Yasmin with every fiber in his being. Anthony felt he waited his entire life for a woman like Yasmin and believed that God surely loved him to bless him with such a fine jewel who he felt adored and loved him just as much as he loved her. Anthony's job kept him on the road extensively managing campaigns in various cities and opening up new offices in several states. On one of his visits, he received a phone call from Yasmin stating that she was pregnant but the cervical cancer from previous years had come out of remission. She was facing extreme dangers and needed to make a hard decision to either save her life or that of their unborn child. Anthony was devastated. He heard what appeared to be the greatest news of his fairytale relationship in one breath while now facing a catastrophic decision in the other. Almost immediately Anthony felt the decision was apparent, he felt that they could always have another baby but there would only be one Yasmin and therefore decided that if needed, they would terminate the pregnancy.

After several doctor visits Yasmin went in for what Anthony thought was a procedure to remove the cancer that resurfaced. However, Yasmin's reluctance to have Anthony present caused speculation and uncertainty for the first time in Anthony's mind. He rushed home after a long stint on the road to be by Yasmin's side but something had changed and he was not sure what it was. Yasmin was very distant and Anthony was puzzled. A week later while Anthony prepared to leave on a business trip, Yasmin delivered what boxers would consider the knockout blow. Anthony and Yasmin's relationship publicly was the epitome of love and life but privately on its last leg as she informed Anthony that she no longer wanted to be in the relationship sending his heart to the bottom of his feet and severing his emotions from his manly nature.

Deception is one of our biggest foes! We are dying from deception. The serpent deceived eve! Eve deceived Adam. There's power in deception—Mo Stegall

Do You Mean What You Say

The fairytale was over and the sneak attack had literally crippled Anthony paralyzing his soul. As Anthony struggled to make the business trip, what kept replaying in his mind was Yasmin's reason for leaving his lifeless spirit to be food for the vultures of men and women he would meet long after the smoke from this dissipated relationship cleared. Yasmin told Anthony that she could not hear the music of their relationship any longer because looking at him would be a constant reminder of the child they lost.

This story is all too familiar to many of you reading this book and equally, the pain that accompanied selfish motives and manipulative mindsets. Anthony suspected from a subtle investigation he conducted that while on a business trip Yasmin had an affair with an ex-boyfriend and it was in fact his baby that she was carrying and not his own. Anthony's mother, a former nurse further confirmed the story when she discovered the procedure that Yasmin had was an abortion not cancer surgery.

Words are more powerful than we could ever imagine and men and women alike engage in dialogue daily without awareness of the power that they possess with their conversations. I recall my grandmother often saying to me "Say what you mean…and mean what you say", a statement that I attempt to live by daily. However, I myself have abused the saying by at times in my life not adhering to the code of ethics as it relates to relationships and saying things I did not mean in order to get what I wanted.

The damage caused by selfish ambitions can last beyond the initial impact so we must be aware of our own actions when building friendships, intimate relationships or professional partnerships. I loved the movie "Jerry McGuire" a 1996 American romantic comedy-drama film starring Tom Cruise, Cuba Gooding, Jr and Renée Zellweger. Written, co-produced, and directed by Cameron Crowe. The film was released in North American theaters on December 13, 1996, distributed by Gracie Films and TriStar Pictures.

Jerry Maguire (Tom Cruise) is a glossy 35-year-old sports agent working for *Sports Management International* (SMI). After suffering a nervous breakdown as a result of stress and a guilty conscience, he writes a mission statement about perceived dishonesty in the sports management business and how he believes that it should be operated. He distributes copies of it, entitled "The Things We Think and Do Not Say: The Future of Our Business". His co-workers are touched by his honesty and greet him with applause, but it is his brute honesty that prompted management to show him the door. It was Jerry's moment with Frank "Cush" Cushman (Jerry O'Connell), a superstar football prospect from Southern Methodist University expected to be #1 in the NFL Draft that moves me the most. Moments after Jerry has experienced a delightful time with his client Rod Tidwell played by Gooding and looking to capitalize on the moment with Cush, he learns by an unexpected phone call from rival agent Bob Sugar that Cush and his father has retracted their promise to sign with his agency. The news baffles him and prompts him to utter the infamous statement, "I'm still sort of moved by your "My word is stronger than oak" thing. Previously, Cush and his father promised Jerry that they would sign with him and if an offer came to the table, they would discuss it with him prior to signing any other contract. However, on signing day before the draft, they signed with his rival.

How many of us have good intentions but often fail to mean what we say or are easily persuaded to go against our stronger than oak word? Since the beginning of time we have had "The Word", this is in reference to God's word but, we are also challenged to carry integrity and good character, which constitutes our word resonating honesty and truth. We should carry the integrity mantle with honor and know as men that we have the power to change how society views us. It pains me when I hear the chatter in circles that "**All MEN CHEAT**" or "**ALL MEN ARE DOGS**" because that is the farthest from the truth. A few bad apples do not spoil the entire bunch, as my grandmother would always say.

What we must do to assure that our word carry weight today is, examine the essentials when it comes to the promises we make, look beyond periodic pleasure and further into the affects of the communicative bonds we may break with empty promises and finally, encompass more self control than our need for self and public acceptance.

What we falter on today with misplaced chatter may very well choke our progress for tomorrow when the whispers resurface.

8 LISTEN & RESPOND

Even a beautiful woman doesn't know what she wants until she sees It.—Hitch

When thinking of the overall operation of men a scripture comes to mind, Mark 4:9 *"and he said unto them, He that hath ears to hear, let him hear."* We tend to listen only with our ears, but there is a deeper kind of listening that we must learn to explore. Listening with the mind and heart is necessary in order to gain insight and understanding and will be pivotal in any relationship we develop.

Gaining understanding is what will allow us to maneuver through a variety of obstacles, important ventures and everyday living that's needed for us to progress and grow. Isn't growth the ultimate goal in life? How can we move forward if we never grow? When we were children, we grew to become young adults and as young adults, we will march into adulthood. Learning to listen more than we speak will allow us to actually hear what is being said, digest what is heard and then follow suit or respond accordingly.

My wife and I during the early stages of our marriage and at various times throughout it have had several disagreements and I noticed that during those disagreements neither of us was listening to the other. Therefore, we had no clue as to how to resolve the issue. We were doing more talking than listening and that method propelled our conversations to turn into full fledge arguments or for the politically correct…**Disagreements**.

Hear, Learn and Follow

As we have matured in our relationship I have often wondered what would have happened or how much time and agony would we have saved had we taken the time to **HEAR, LEARN** and **FOLLOW?**

Hearing requires an attentiveness that is not concerned with getting its point across or initiating an agenda that is primarily self-centered. Hearing says I am slowly disseminating what is being said so that I may digest its content and context in order to tentatively address the issue or concern appropriately.

The popular game of talk and repeat, where a statement is made and then passed along to several people to determine how much of the original statement remains intact by the time it gets to the end of the line is intriguing because, it never makes it to the end of the line in its original state. Somehow, between participants, the phrase or statement is altered. Many stand perplexed as to how this happens repeatedly and the answer is very simple…someone did not apply their listening skills completely or their listening digestive system is flawed. Regardless of what the issue is, in the game the information is distorted and flawed.

Learning suggests that information given is retained and applied. When I was in the third grade, I remember having a special teacher to assist me with learning math because something about multiplication was perplexing me and I was not learning at the level of my peers. It would take me longer than the time required to digest how one number multiplied by the other would yield the answer. I cannot tell you why my brain was not calculating the problem and producing an answer. Many of us in our relationships are not adequately able to digest the issues and therefore are deficient in supplying or rendering an answer to assist us and or our mate resolve all the subtle issues of life and relationships. Therefore, we are either crippling our relationships or sabotaging them altogether.

I am a stickler about getting clarity even with the simplest things and at times, it drives my wife crazy. I ask a host of questions because a part of me is still that third grader who has complications with adhering, digesting, and comprehending the complexities of communication.

Two-time Academy Award winner Denzel Washington ignites a masterpiece of mayhem in the powerful action-thriller "Man on Fire" as CIA operative John Casey who has given up on life until his friend gets him a job as a bodyguard to a nine-year-old girl named Pita Ramos who is in danger of being kidnapped by rebels. Washington's character often posed a simple but intriguing statement when questioning his suspects; he would say, "Explain it to me as if I was a two-year old". He was so inclined to understand that he wanted the text simplified to an extent that a child could comprehend. We must simplify the complexities of our relationships with an understanding of what is being said and what we are hearing, coupled with, digesting what is heard and, taking that comprehension and applying it to how we respond. No matter how right we think we are, we must always be careful to stop and listen to others. The extra time and effort can save us pain and trouble in the end.

Following, means to pursue or run after to cling or overtake, to imitate, strive for or attend. Many are in pursuit of a meaningful relationship and are striving to be intimately entwined in a love cycle that continues to produce fruitful memories versus asthmatic nightmares. I have learned that how we model our relationships often determines the types of relationships we will actually produce. I never saw my mother and father together intimately or in a loving environment and I could not understand why but I would later learn that they were not together as a couple. I was not able to model a loving two-parent environment therefore, I never learned prior to getting married how to operate in that type of environment. It seemed that there were several decks stacked against me, my father was not present, my mother could only teach me from a limited perspective and friends who were not privy to a single-parent home could not lend support or provide guidance and advice.

As we continue to grow and develop relationships throughout our lives, we must learn to listen attentively and respond accordingly. Women have a different aptitude for learning than men and therefore, what we both hear is not what is being said and what is being said isn't necessarily what is heard. The key to obtaining and maintaining successful relationships be it personal or professional is listening and responding. Listen twice as much as we talk and respond with a conscientious discourse that verbalize attentiveness and, comprehension. Paying careful attention is hard work. It involves focusing our mind, body and senses.

PART TWO: HER VOICE

⏻ Power Point to Ponder

A great deal of miscommunication in relationships is due to more words broadcasted than digested. Listen twice as much as you speak, be attentive and train your ear to hear the silent tones of his/her inner thoughts reverberating in the movement of their actions.

❓ Question to Consider

Are your lips saying what you really mean? Are you attentive to details that may go unseen or heard? Is your love cycle one that creates fruitful memories or asthmatic nightmares?

💎 Jewel Tip

Deception impairs your vision of reality and prohibits you from walking in truth or receiving it.

POWER NOTES:

PART THREE

HER FLATTERY

THE POISON IN HER HEART WILL KILL YOU

A heart that plots evil, feet that race to do wrong, a false witness who pours out lies, a person who sows discord in a family.

Proverbs 6:18-19

We discussed in an earlier chapter about the dangers of being poisoned, how it effects cause serious injury or death. We never really learn what causes a woman to act with evil intent or malice. I would be inclined to believe that something or someone may have hurt her at some point in her life and in her possibly hiding her hurt she prevented adequate healing.

The 1996 dark comedy-romance film "A Thin Line Between Love and Hate" directed and co-written by Martin Lawrence, who also stars in the film as nightclub manager Darnell, a perpetual playboy and hopeless male chauvinist. Darnell is a crude-but-smooth talker and lady's man who does not take no for an answer. He works for a nightclub called *Chocolate City* and aspires to be its owner. He trades VIP privileges at the club for favors from women. Though he is an expert at conning women, he sometimes worries about what his childhood sweetheart Mia (Regina King) thinks of his adventures.

When the classy, elegant Brandi (Lynn Whitfield) steps out of a limousine to enter the club, Darnell feels that he has met his ultimate prize. She rejects his come-ons, which only fuels his appetite. He pursues her by showing up with flowers at her real estate office. He finally wins, only to find out that he is really in love with Mia. Nevertheless, Brandi does not take kindly to rejection, and becomes an obsessed femme fatale stalking him, even taking all four wheels off his SUV to ground him from his rounds. Cutting off his engagement to Mia is not enough to satisfy Brandi, who finally administers Darnell's punishment for his misogyny. Darnell quickly learns the hard way that when you "play", you have to "pay." The film ends with an injured Darnell in the hospital pondering over what happened to him and deciding to change. Before the movie fades to black, a mug shot of Brandi flashes and Darnell's voice reverberates saying, "Damn I'm truly sorry about what happened to Brandi I hope she lands on her feet, but they better make damn sure they fix that dent in her heart before they let her out".

I would imagine that many of you who may have had an encounter with a woman scarred from a previous relationship or an insensitive man can attest to Brandi from the movie. Brandi, like most women who pour their hearts into a man who is not ready to commit to a long-term relationship or any type of relationship that requires monogamy, often will suffer from the venomous heartache hibernating in her heart after a devastating encounter. A night full of passion can give you a lifetime of pain and the line between a woman loving you or hating you is dental floss thin. Although we cannot always shelter every woman in the world from heartache and pain, what we must do as men in order for her to become the jewel we desperately need is begin to prepare for surgery as if we were surgeons.

Many are in need of open-heart surgery and do not know it and in order for restoration to commence, we must address the possibility of becoming heart surgeons.

Preparing For Surgery

In 1995, I was involved in an accident that fractured my tibia and fibula and required surgery to repair. Because my injury was serious and very urgent, I did not have adequate time to mentally or physically prepare for it. Researchers say that preparing for surgery is quite an event and unless it is an emergency as in my case, you should try and find out all you can about the condition you are being treated for and the operation being planned. Ask your surgeon or nurse about details of the surgery, the risks involved, potential complications and how they will be managed, quality of life afterwards and, anything else you would like to know.

I believe it's one thing to have a condition and need surgery and another to need surgery but have yet to detect the condition in order to obtain the proper surgery necessary. Many are in need of heart surgery and have yet to realize it. I recall, when I was in the fourth grade, I had a huge fascination with WWE wrestling. I conjured a few friends together and we proceeded to have a battle royal rumble in the jungle type outdoor wrestling match. While beating on one of my friends he throws me out of the makeshift ring (concrete porch with metal railing) unto our makeshift arena floor where we pretended that ten thousand adoring fans were screaming our name and cheering for the death match between its two biggest rivals. We proceeded to beat on each other with play-by-play commentary depicting every move and as we geared up for the final move outside the ring, something went terribly wrong. I grabbed my rival and put him in the death defying hook neck lock and proceeded to drop to the floor when he suddenly pulled out and pushed me back I heard a snap, crackle and a pop and when I rolled over I saw that my pants had a hole in them. I could see red, white, and blue and it was not the good ole American flag either.

I had cut myself on a broken bottle and it sliced my leg open. I hobbled back to my house; I was convinced that all I needed was a band-aid and a few gauze patches to clean the wound. The injury was much more serious than I wanted to believe and I ended up needing sixty-five stitches and clamps to seal the wound.

I was like many of you who have wounded hearts and, somehow with all the pain you wrestle with daily, weekly, monthly and the visible damage, feel like you can place a band-aid on a hatchet wound.

I realized that it was my fear of my mother seeing this injury and knowing that it was caused by my horseplay that frightened me into believing the injury was not as serious as it actually was. What are your drawbacks to seeking and receiving the healing you need in order to be the man or woman that you were designed to be? I believe that if you do not acknowledge the events that may have caused your injury you will not only continuously suffer from its affects but will never be inclined to fix it. A wise man once shared with me that we cannot fix what we are unwilling to face. God aims to heal every broken place, mend every broken piece and restore you back to prominence; you must decide today that you want to be complete again.

I laughed at the old tale about the lovable character we all learned about in elementary school named "Humpty Dumpty". Humpty

Dumpty is a character in an English language nursery rhyme, probably originally a riddle and one of the best known in the English-speaking world. The rhyme went as so:

Humpty Dumpty sat on a wall;
Humpty Dumpty had a great fall.
All the King's horses
And all the King's men
Couldn't put Humpty together again!

Many of us are like Humpty Dumpty. We have been broken to a point that all of those who sincerely love us seem to have a task helping us get life back together again. Healing first begins with us making an informed decision that we are in need of care and allowing the doctors to give us the proper surgery necessary to repair what is damaged. Afterwards, we must mentally prepare for the process of regaining trust and understanding that every person we will meet in our lives are not identical to the one that caused the damage.

I believe that if Samson were given the opportunity to survive the destruction, he would have learned a valuable lesson about inspecting what he expected from Delilah versus allowing her persistence to wear him down to a point of giving away what God anointed sacred and set apart to be used for his glory. No matter where you are at this moment in your life God is a restorer and has provided various mechanisms that can and will assist you with your healing process. Commit to obtaining the necessary surgery needed and get ready for a wonderful ride back to the victory stand.

10 THE BODYGUARD

Keep thy heart with all diligence; for out of it are the issues of life.
Proverbs 4:23

The Bodyguard is a 1992 American romantic-thriller film starring Kevin Costner and the late Whitney Houston. Costner stars as a former Secret Service Agent turned bodyguard who is hired to protect Houston's character, a music star, from an unknown stalker. Rachel Marron (Houston) is an Oscar-nominated music superstar who is being stalked and sent death threats. Frank Farmer (Costner) is a former Secret Service Special Agent who served as part of the presidential protection detail during Presidents Jimmy Carter and Ronald Reagan's presidencies. He is now a highly successful private professional bodyguard who protects corporate VIP's. Rachel's manager, Bill Devaney, hires him to protect her after she receives a number of threats against her life and a small bomb detonates in her dressing room. Frank is haunted by the fact that he was not there when Reagan was shot because he was off duty at the time.

The film follows Rachel's life through her career and family. The film's dramatic outlay has viewers on the edge of their seats throughout but, when the hit man breaks into the house and Nikki tries to stop him, he shoots and kills her before escaping. Frank ensures that his father, who is armed with a large caliber revolver, has secured the rest of the group on the second floor of the house then, Frank pursues the killer out into the woods. Frank shoots at the assassin but the hit man escapes through the dark woods. Frank learns the next day from his Secret Service colleagues that they have apprehended the stalker and were interviewing him when Nikki was shot. After Nikki's funeral and a few days later, Rachel goes to the Academy Awards because she is nominated for best actress. The assassin attempts to murder Rachel again with a gun hidden inside a video camera, when she accepts her award for Best Actress. Frank jumps in front of her to save her life, and is shot himself. Frank manages to shoot the hit man through the camera lenses right through the eye before losing consciousness. The hit man turns out to be his friend and former Secret Service coworker Greg Portman (Tomas Arana). Tony (Mike Starr) loses an eye during the melee, having had it gouged out by Portman, but both he and Frank survive their injuries. Frank sees Rachel off at the airport. His arm is in a sling. Frank has arranged for another protection detail to augment Tony who is back on the job wearing a black eye patch. Frank's duty having been fulfilled by successfully protecting Rachel, they part with a kiss.

    I felt setting up this chapter with that story was necessary because it truly depicts what I will share. We often are smitten with feelings or emotions, anger or frustration, love and even lust but few understand the need to have what Whitney Houston's character in the film needed and that was a Bodyguard. The bodyguard protected her from danger but also shielded her from influence within her circle. How many of us need a personal bodyguard to shield us from the onslaught of our emotions in the relationships we engage? How many of us would be in a better place of healing from the years of hurt, manipulation, disappointments or deceit we have experienced in our lives? The bodyguard protects us and advises us on decisions that place us in the best place of safety from others and ourselves.

The bible says in Proverbs 4:23 *"Keep thy heart with all diligence; for out of it are the issues of life".* What does this passage of scripture really mean? Our heart-our feelings of love and desire dictates to a great extent how we live because we always find time to do what we enjoy. Solomon tells us to guard our heart above all else, making sure we concentrate on those desires that will keep us on the right path. Make sure your affections lead you in the right direction. Put boundaries on your desires: Do not go after everything you see. Look straight ahead, keep your eyes fixed on your goal, and do not get sidetracked on desires that lead to wrong choices or sin.

The protector you need is discernment and time. Discernment helps you inspect what you expect from relationships, business deals, friends, etc. and time allows you to see the representative I spoke about in an earlier chapter unveil the genuine plan versus the one presented when you first meet. Be careful and allow your bodyguard to do the job you have enlisted it to do…and that is protecting you.

THE BLACK HOLE 11

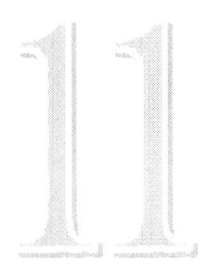

For there is nothing hidden which will not be revealed, nor has anything been kept secret but that it should come to light.
Mark 4:22

Wikipedia defines a black hole as a region of space-time from which nothing, not even light, can escape. The theory of general relativity predicts that a sufficiently compact mass will deform space-time to form a black hole. Around a black hole there is a mathematically defined surface called an event horizon that marks the point of no return. It's called "black" because it absorbs all the light that hits the horizon, reflecting nothing, just like a perfect black body in thermodynamics.

When we view relationships, we often never see those black hole type relationships that invisibly haul us in to a point of no return. We become emotionally engulfed, spiritually connected, and at times financially invested long before we realize that it has sucked the life out of us and has rendered us no return on our investment. Now I am not suggesting that in every relationship we should expect all that we put into it to be returned back to us; I am simply saying we should get something from the relationship at some level.

A vacuum cleaner is designed to suck things in without releasing anything out and many of us may have been involved with a Black Hole type relationship that has literally sucked us so far in that it has become increasingly difficult to see the hand right in front of our faces. I like to call this…**The Blackout!**

The Blackout

Many have believed over the years that wearing all black or dark colors disguises unwanted fat or paints the illusion that weight loss has occurred but it is a deception because although nothing was done to actually lose the weight, wearing black makes you appear slimmer.

Truth is black is often used to hide things. When there is a power outage, it is entitled a blackout. In wartime or in preparation for an expected war a blackout is the practice of collectively minimizing outdoor light. In addition, upwardly directed or reflected light. This was done in the 20th century to prevent crews of enemy aircraft from being able to navigate to their targets simply by sight; for example, during the London Blitz of 1940.

In broadcasting, the term blackout refers to the non-airing of television or radio programming in a certain media market. It is particularly prevalent in the broadcasting of sporting events, although other television or radio programs may be blacked out as well.

Media blackout refers to the censorship of news related to a certain topic, particularly in mass media, for any reason. A media blackout may be voluntary or may in some countries, be enforced by the government or state. The latter case is controversial in peacetime, as some regard it as a human rights violation and repression of free speech. Press blackout is a similar term, but refers specifically to printed media.

The dark side of relationships are the most difficult to assess and digest because they depict hidden unresolved issues that may be a detriment to any future relationships if not resolved. Black is always seen as a mystery. The grim reaper wears a black robe, and a thief commits his robbery wearing all black. The reasoning for this is black has been seen as a cover up for things and therefore hides what we do not want seen.

This is very much the case with many of us. Often we will wear shades to a funeral or for personalities (celebrities) in public when making appearances and, it is all to cover or shield us from something or someone. Does wearing shades truly shield us from being seen? Absolutely not but, they allow us to conceal a part of us that we feel needs protecting. We are shielding ourselves within the black hole of our emotional trauma or for some, hiding ourselves from the truth in the relationship.

I myself have fallen in the black hole of love, temptation, life and the ambiguous proclamation that persists when living a lie haunted me until I realized that covering up my issues was not going to allow me to submerge from the nightfall of my decisions unscathed. I knew eventually the scripture I read for years would manifest and that scripture stated in **Luke 8:17** *For all that is secret will eventually be brought into the open, and everything that is concealed will be brought to light and made known to all.*

What a dilemma! Not exactly, I was left with what everyone on earth is given...A Choice! I could choose to continue to harbor my deceitful endeavors or I could seek help and allow God to use the UV lamp to nurse me back to health.

Using the UV Lamp

But all things become visible when they are exposed by the light, for everything that becomes visible is light. Ephesians 5:13

Ultraviolet (UV) light is electromagnetic radiation with a wavelength shorter than that of visible light, but longer than X-rays, in the range 10 nanometers to 400 nanometers, and energies from 3 eV to 124 eV. *(I do not expect you to understand what I just said because I don't)*. It is named because the spectrum consists of electromagnetic waves with frequencies higher than those that humans identify as the color violet. These frequencies are invisible to humans, but visible to a number of insects and birds. They are also indirectly visible, by causing fluorescent materials to glow with visible light.

A black light, Wood's light, or UV light is a lamp that emits long-wave UV radiation and very little visible light. Fluorescent black lights are typically made in the same fashion as normal fluorescent lights, except that a different phosphor is used on the inside of the tube. This emits UV instead of visible light, and the clear glass envelope of the bulb may be replaced by a deep-bluish-purple glass called Wood's glass, a nickel-oxide–doped glass, which blocks almost all visible light above 400 nanometers. The color of such lamps are often referred to in the lighting industry as "black light blue" or "BLB", to distinguish them from UV lamps used in "bug zapper" insect traps that do not have the blue Wood's glass.

In order for us to expose those deep-rooted things or secrets that are restraining us from receiving the abundance of life, we must utilize God's UV lamp to see the things within us that are not visible by the natural eye. A secret is only a secret to those who do not know that it exists and for many of us we have something that no one knows about including our closest friends and family members. I am not suggesting that you share with the world your deep dark secrets in order to be free. I am merely suggesting that you allow the UV lamp of God's word to demonstrate to you its love, restoring power, and reconciliation to your rightful place in the kingdom.

Again, I repeat we cannot fix anything that we are unwilling to face and those things in which we sweep under the rug are the roadblocks that are keeping us from living a righteous life according to the scriptures that we believe.

12 WHAT IS SHE REALLY ATTRACTED TO?

Beauty may fade but the anointing along with the gifts of the spirit will outlive even the one who carries it!

Have you ever wondered what women were attracted to when showing interest in you or alternatively, asked yourself why you were the chosen one versus the other available candidates? I have often wondered and asked myself those questions and have come to the conclusion that at times it isn't our handsome face, sculptured body or lavish lifestyle that attracts women to us. It could be our prowess to succeed, determination to make a difference, anointing to influence others, or simply the sincere passion for loving the woman we meet. Whatever it is that draws women to men and causes them to engage in dialogue that may lead to something sufficient we must all agree that they are engrossed by something.

Contrary to the myth about women that many men believe regarding equality, I have learned that when God created Eve for Adam that he made them equally important and God forms and equips men and women for various tasks but all these tasks lead to the same goal-honoring God. Man gives life to woman; woman gives life to the world. Each role carries exclusive privileges.

God gave marriage as a gift to Adam and Eve. They were created perfect for each other. Many of you are thinking if this is the case then why are there so many divorces. I believe we must define or identify the reasons as to why men and women are attracted to certain types and pursue relationships with each other.

I have often used the term "Inspecting What You Expect", and truly believe this may be the leading cause of why so many end up in the whirlwind of relationship turmoil, heartache, and frustration. Many of us jump into things without proper research and therefore have no awareness of what it will actually take to attain, relinquish, maintain, etc. and that approach has cost us a great deal of time, energy and effort. We must conduct a more thorough inspection of the type of relationship, woman, career and or position in society we wish to obtain or we will continue the cycle of repetitious reward.

Supping with Naomi

Many of you have heard the wonderful story of Ruth and Naomi, two women whose stories were woven together so closely that they are almost inseparable. Their story was a great example and model of good relationships. They shared deep sorrow, great affection for each other and, an overriding commitment to the God of Israel. Although they were close female friends, my analogy will assist you in identifying the type of friend you need your woman to be to assist with nurturing you back to health.

Naomi was kind, trustworthy and filled with moral integrity. She had a strong relationship with God in spite of the tragedy she experienced in losing her husband and all of her possessions. Naomi was the epitome of a true friend and she did what a majority of us don't or won't do, she denied what she wanted to assure that her daughter-in-law Ruth had everything that she needed. Naomi created a relationship where the greatest bond was faith in God, strong mutual commitment, and one in which each person tried to do what was best for the other.

How many of us have relationships that are foundationally built on these premises and have little room for frivolous behavior destroying the friendship? Ruth gave up security and children to care for Naomi although Naomi had no other sons for her to marry. The mate that you pursue or entertain must be someone whose agenda is to care for you out of sincerity versus what you can provide for them.

Being Her Boaz

Heroes are easier to admire than to define. Heroes simply do the right thing at the right time, whether or not they realize the impact their action will have. Boaz was a man of his word, sensitive to those in need. He cared for his workers, possessed a keen sense of responsibility and integrity, and was a successful and shrewd businessperson. The one quality that stands out in a hero is that he has a tendency to think of others before thinking of himself. It is impossible for you to be the man that your woman will essentially need if you possess a selfish spirit. Boaz was a hero. In his dealings with other people, he was always sensitive to their needs. His words to his employees, relatives, and others were colored with kindness. He offered help openly, not grudgingly. Boaz not only did what was right; he also did it right away.

Women are often quoted as looking for their "Boaz" but many are not equipped to handle what he may offer. Men must equip themselves with the proper mentality and heart to become the men that women need to build healthy relationships and families.

You become like Boaz by putting the needs of others ahead of your own, a keen sense of responsibility and integrity and be able to provide for the woman that you desire to date and marry. Provision is not always financial. A number of men believe that simply having a great paying job is enough to place him in the category of being a provider, but women need more than just a financial safe haven. Women need affection, attention, love, care, a listening ear, quality time and many, more things that money cannot buy.

Boaz understood what was necessary to place Ruth in the best position to become his wife. He sincerely cared for her despite the uphill battle that preceded her.

Being the man that she will essentially desire will require you to become desirable. This means allowing God to develop you into a man with sincerity, heart, character and, integrity.

SLIPPERY WHEN WET 13

It is much easier to fall on black ice than white snow, for one display itself vividly while the other conceals its identity.

Have you ever driven over a bridge and noticed a sign that read "Slippery When Wet" or been a grocery store after clean up and the clerk has put down the caution sign to alert shoppers of the danger areas that may cause a fall? All of those were warnings to make the driver or consumer aware of the problems that were up ahead and if they did not heed to the forewarnings certain dangers may await.

We all have seen these signs and have equally seen someone ignore them only to walk directly into the danger zone. Some suffer minor injuries and others, serious injuries or death.

If we could be honest for a moment (*since it is just you and I here and no one else in the room we can talk* **"uno a uno"**), how many times have we seen or sensed warning signs in life as well as relationships of any sort and properly ignored them? It is those preeminent dangers that if detected early enough could prevent or alter many outcomes. The issue with a number of us is that we often ignore the caution sign that says this relationship, business venture or career choice is slippery when wet, meaning when something hits its surface that is not easily managed that substance could cause damage.

The flattery of a woman can be exhilarating and dangerous at the same time. I often say, if we never discover a person's objective it may be impossible to determine if the relationship is genuine or artificial. If a man's primary goal is to sleep with a woman and he accomplishes that goal on the first date or the fifteenth date nonetheless, the goal has been attained. The problem with this scenario is if the woman doesn't make the time to learn of this objective she will become bewildered when his attitude towards her shifts to merely going through the motions versus building a healthy relationship. Vice versa with men. If we are not focused on the objectives of the people we encounter in life. We may find ourselves continually in similar predicaments as before because the motives never changed yet the players in the game have.

Knowing someone's purpose for engaging with you is vital to the growth and development of that relationship. We can better gauge the dynamics of where a relationship may lead if we have a keen eye on its purpose. Men and women often go into relationships with a purpose yet very few inspect the other's purpose prior to allowing the relationship to flourish. Our desires are what have led many down a slippery slope of deceit, manipulation and heartache.

It's amazing how the odds of you falling on a slippery step increases daily with every interaction. When we are engaged in certain activities, a perilous encounter may render us helpless in the end.

Do not allow yourself to fall into diverse temptations or hazardous relationships due to your negligence. Examine each scenario carefully and proceed with extreme caution because nothing spells demise like driving on a bridge with bald tires when sleet has fallen and you are well aware that black ice exists.

PART THREE: HER FLATTERY

⏻ Power Point to Ponder

The heart can be deceptive for out of it flow the issues of life. Some relationship encounters may be poisonous and hazardous, monitor what goes in and what is coming out. We all have valuables that need protecting and implementing a system that allows your valuables to remain secure is vitally important. What you can't see will harm you and place you in a venerable position therefore, use caution and adhere to the warning signs.

❓ Questions to Consider

Are you telling others what you believe they want to hear to get what you want? Are you allowing God to make you desirable? Are you adhering to the visible warning signs or ignoring them?

💎 Jewel Tip

What you give today to win his/her affection is what they will expect tomorrow to retain their love. You must be prepared to invest long-term.

POWER NOTES:

PART FOUR

HER TOUCH

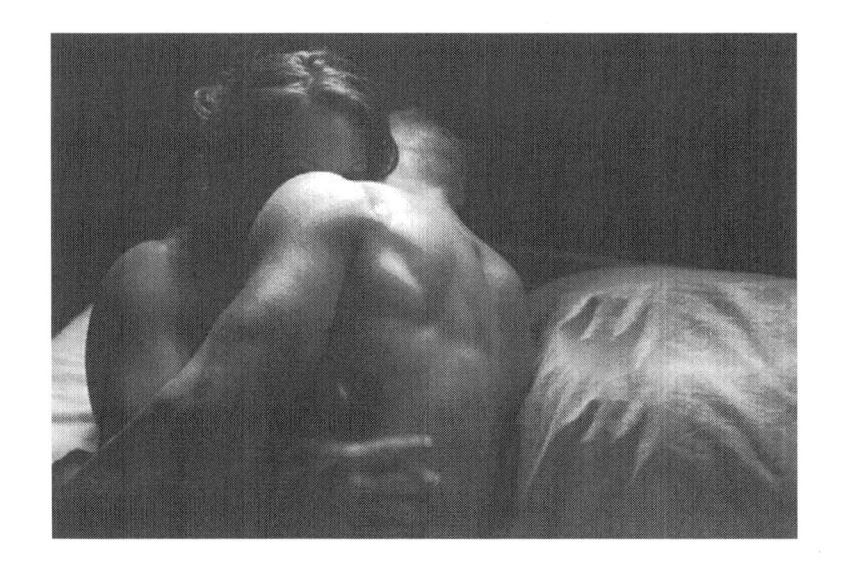

14 HER HAND HIS HEART

Hearts of deception tend to tie Hands of love to an illusion…Painting a delicate picture of persistence pursued by infatuation making it a venerable target.

Delilah played a minor role in Samson's life but her effect was devastating, for she influenced him to betray his special calling from God. Motivated by greed, Delilah used her persistence to wear down Samson. His infatuation with her made Samson a venerable target. Delilah valued money more than relationships and ultimately betrayed the man who trusted her. She utterly gave him her hand and led him into a den of thieves waiting to steal his strength and crush the thing that Samson allowed to lead him….his **HEART!!!**

We addressed the dangers of leading with your heart and how the bible instructs us to guard our hearts because out of it flow the issues of life. When God created woman she was pulled from the left rib of man so that as his wife, she may guard his heart from the troubles that the world would offer him. She was sworn in as the heart police vowing to protect and serve his heart with every fiber of her being.

Many men are reading wondering where that woman lives, inbox me and I will gladly send you her address. For the small remnant of you who are saying that you use to be married to that woman but there seems to be a disconnect because it appears that she no longer desires to protect and serve, I have an anecdote.

{Station Break}

If your woman is protecting and serving, you at this moment and you have no issue you may skip to the next chapter or continue reading and possibly learn something you did not know already

{Now Back To Your Regular Scheduled Program}

Delilah ruled Samson with her hand. She knew his heart rested in it and she understood the power she possessed because her motives were not pure or focused on building a genuine long term relationship with him she utilized that power to destroy him. I often have wondered reading similar stories online or in the paper, how could something so precious and sweet, tender and eloquent, soft and beautiful be so evil and manipulative and have such malice in its heart that it doesn't consider for one moment the damage that its decisions will cause.

1Timothy 6:10 says, *"For the love of money is a root of all kinds of evil. Some people, eager for money, have wandered from the faith and pierced themselves with many grief's."*

The Delilah that you have encountered in your life was concerned about what she could conjure in her hands that she had very little concern about the hole that she would leave in your heart. The scriptures suggest the number one issue is that she wandered from the faith and maybe her heart was pierced with grief from a previous relationship and she never healed, therefore, making it impossible for her to give to you out of her shattered and empty cupboard.

Dating Many Delilah's Before Meeting Deborah

Unlike Delilah, the bible's character, Deborah was opposite. Delilah, cared only for herself while Deborah was not power hungry, she wanted to serve God. The bible, says whenever praise came her way, she gave God the credit. She was a fierce and very intelligent leader who accomplish great amounts of work without direct involvement because she knew how to work through other people. She was able to see the big picture that often escapes those directly involved, so she made for an excellent mediator, adviser and, planner. The skills that Deborah possessed to lead were great but none more than her remarkable relationship with God and that alone set her apart from Delilah.

Her story shows that she was not power hungry. She wanted to serve God. She did not deny or resist her position in the culture as a woman and wife, but she never allowed herself to be hindered by it either. She demonstrated that God could use people who are willing to be led by him.

Deborah carried a greater respect for her assignment, her family and, her husband because she included the one ingredient that mattered most…God! In your search for a mate, you will need one that has the following:

Relationship with God-This will set your mate apart from every other candidate and set a tone for the relationship that will only increase with time.

Unselfish Motives- Having a genuine concern for others and placing their needs above your own will allow you to progress and position you to receive God's choice blessings.

Ability to Plan, Direct and Delegate- A great leader understands his/her success is predicated on their ability to make concise decisions, delegate and build effectively.

ENTRAPMENT OF THE COOKIE JAR

(THE SEX CHAPTER)

To be ensnared by a grasp stronger than your will to fight it, discernment to sense it, or power to overcome it may be classified as an addiction and require treatment.

In criminal law, entrapment is conduct by a law enforcement agent inducing a person to commit an offense that the person would otherwise have been unlikely to commit. In the 1999 blockbuster hit movie "Entrapment", Sean Connery and Catherine Zeta-Jones lead an all-star cast and audience on a suspense thriller full of chess moves. Virginia "Gin" Baker (Catherine Zeta-Jones) is an investigator for Waverly Insurance. Robert "Mac" MacDougal (Connery) is an international art thief. A priceless Rembrandt painting is stolen from an office one night. Gin is sent to investigate Mac as the chief suspect. She tries to entrap him with a proposition, claiming that she is a thief herself. She promises that she will help him steal a priceless Chinese mask from the well-guarded Bedford Palace. They travel to Scotland and plan the complicated theft at Mac's hideout: an isolated castle. While Mac is busy making final preparations, Gin contacts her boss, Hector Cruz (Will Patton), and informs him of Mac's whereabouts. Little does she know that the island is bugged, allowing Mac to eavesdrop on their conversation.

In many jurisdictions, entrapment is a possible defense against criminal liability. However, there is no entrapment where a person is ready and willing to break the law. The government agents merely provide what appears to be a favorable opportunity for the person to commit the crime.

We have often found ourselves in some compromising positions when it comes to the opposite sex and those positions are the ones we do not do on family Twister night. The more important question is not if we allow ourselves to become entrapped by the subtle, sensual and, sexy aura of a woman but why are we continually engaging with no forethought of the consequences that ensue?

Many of you may say what is the big deal, everyone engages in pre-marital sex! Oh! You did not know that is the alter ego of the term entrapment of the cookie jar! It is a term of endearment and has caused many empires to crumble, marriages to fold, and has left many of lives shattered.

I often wondered why God designed sex and limited it to marriage only or why sexual desires must be placed under God's control. After all, once we entered into young adult and adulthood we are of sound mind and overtly sexually laced body right? I did a bit of digging and found a few interesting scriptures that may shed a brighter light on why God created his laws for premarital sex and why he says that sex is not freedom but enslavement.

God's original idea for sex was outlined during the early biblical days when prostitution was raging in every other religion. Many religions included prostitution as an integral part of its worship services. God said that prostitution made a mockery of his original idea for sex, treating sex as an isolated physical act rather than an act of commitment to another. Outside of marriage, sex destroys relationships, within marriage if approached with the right attitude; it can be a relationship builder. God frequently had to warn people against the practice of extramarital sex.

God created sex for procreation, pleasure and as an expression of love between a husband and wife. Sexual experience must be limited to the marriage relationship to avoid hurting our relationship with God, our relationships with others and ourselves.

I have not always lived by the laws according to the bible and I never truly understood how sexing someone at the consent of both parties was causing hurt, but I have since learned how sex affects us unknowingly and literally eats at the fibers of our being like a cancer.

Cookie Monster

Cookie Monster is a Muppet on the children's television show *Sesame Street*. He is best known for his voracious appetite and his famous eating phrases: "Me want cookie!", "Me eat cookie!", and "Om nom nom nom" (said through a mouth full of food). He often eats anything and everything, including danishes, donuts, lettuce, apples, bananas, as well as normally inedible objects. However, as his name suggests, his preferred food is cookies.

The book *Jim Henson's Designs and Doodles* explains Cookie Monster's origin as follows: "In 1966, Henson drew three monsters that ate cookies and appeared in a General Foods commercial that featured three crunchy snack foods: Wheels, Crowns and Flutes. Each snack was represented by a different monster. These monsters had big appetites for the snack foods (like cookies) they were named after.

This narrative is important because he correlates with how we as men act at times when we observe a beautiful, intelligent or sexy woman. As Cookie Monsters, we possess a healthy appetite for an assortment of women who in some cases are mere objects of our affection therefore, demonstrating God's concern as he stated throughout the bible relating to the cookie jar.

Sweet Tooth

Cookie Monster's appetite could be equated to the term that we often use when we are craving something sweet a *"Sweet Tooth"*. A sweet tooth is defined as having a strong appetite for sweet food. Our cravings are due to what we have fed our appetite primarily meaning if we feed our mind sexual thoughts by viewing certain pictures that depict women in a sexual nature, watch televised images of women either naked or scantily clothe, and engage in risqué conversations that arouses our manhood and stimulates our desires triggering our sex organs to act. If we do not monitor our sugar intake, we will continue to crave cookies like a monster aggressively pursuing to soothe our sweet tooth.

How to Stop Sugar Cravings

We often find ourselves over indulging in several cookie jars. While our spirit-man is shooting flares in the middle of the ocean screaming for the National Guard to rescue him from the lake of lustful love, our flesh is at the infamous former Studio 54 in New York having a party like those thrown back in the late 70's and early 80's.

Holly Little, a certified personal trainer stated on Spark People, an online resource guide, that there isn't a single cure-all to the sweet tooth epidemic, but I would have to disagree. A remedy for curing sugar craving may not have yet to be discovered but I have personally found that God's word heals and cures all things. So regardless, if you are a habitual sweet tooth professional or an amateur cookie jar bandit here are a few things you can do to combat those cravings.

Find a Substitute: You must supplement your sexual appetite with a substitute that is strong enough to combat the cravings i.e. God's word. **Judges 16:15** *"Then Delilah pouted, "How can you tell me, 'I love you,' when you don't share your secrets with me? You've made fun of me three times now, and you still haven't told me what makes you so strong!"*

Samson was deceived because he wanted to believe Delilah's lies. How you can keep your desire for love and sexual pleasure from deceiving you:

1. You must decide what kind of person you will love before passion takes over. Determine whether a person's character and faith in God are as desirable as his or her physical appearance.
2. Because, most of the time you spend with your spouse will not involve sex, your companion's personality, temperament and commitment to solve problems must be as gratifying as his or her kisses.
3. Be patient. The second look often reveals what is beneath the pleasant appearance and attentive touch.

Fast and Pray: Fasting will allow you to seek God for healing and demonstrates your dependency on him to heal you. Hunger pangs would reinforce your penitence and remind you of your weakness allowing God to strengthen you through his word to overcome your sexual sickness.

Set Daily Goals: If you don't enlist a plan to get free and stay free you will find yourself back in the cookie jar enslaved to its desires. **Habakkuk 2:2** says, "Then the LORD said to me, "Write my answer plainly on tablets, so that a runner can carry the correct message to others." Writing out your plan will assist you in seeing the journey ahead but empower you to keep running towards the finish line.

Enlist Accountability Partners: Having someone or a group of people who understands God's way of living holding you accountable to the lifestyle you will to live while serving him will help keep you on schedule to living sin free. Remember temptation will always be present but your ability to resist is contingent upon the power that you have inwardly because of God's word working on the inside of you. **1 Thessalonians 5:11** *"Wherefore comfort yourselves together, and edify one another, even as also ye do."*

Create an Environment of Healing: You must create healthy environments that allow your spirit to operate as God desires versus feeding your flesh. If you do all of the above but keep the same unhealthy environment of friends who engage in sex frivolously, watch sexually driven content on television, listen to music that induces sexual thoughts or continuously engage in conversations that promote sexual suggestive behavior, you will find yourself in the sex pool again…I repeat AGAIN and AGAIN!!!

Proverbs 7:25-27 is a clear indication of the dangers of dipping in the cookie jar as it says, *"Do not let your heart turn to her ways or stray into her paths. Many are the victims she has brought down; her slain are a mighty throng. Her house is a highway to the grave, leading down to the chambers of death."* There are definite steps to avoid sexual sins. We must not only focus on the moment-focus on the future. Today's thrill may lead to tomorrow's ruin.

16 SHE'LL NEVER BE MORE THAN YOUR MISTRESS

Fans will find another favorite when the lights have gone dim on your career but friends will sit in the dark with you!

Many have been programmed to believe that life is tough and although I agree with the fact that many aspects of life will not be as endearing as others, life itself once we understand our role and position isn't tough at all. There is no such thing as tough, there is trained and untrained we must determine which one we are.

If we were trained to believe that it was standard issued to have a woman on the side from our wife, most likely that is what many of us have done. We often look at children and wonder why they are the way they are and researchers have concluded that their behavior is often times modeled. What did you see your father or male influence do as it pertained to women? Who were the people who showed you that womanizing was a sport and that you should train to be the best and go after the top prize? ==Many of those questions we tend to ignore because we would rather live a life of lies than face decisive moments.== Going from woman to woman or having a plethora of women at one time is a bit taxing on not only the body but the mind as well.

For those of us who may have been absent from civilization the past four thousand or so years let me explain what a mistress is so that you may either recognize when you observe one in action, or, understand the role you are playing or, the one you have issued to someone else.

A mistress is a long-term female lover and companion who is not married to her partner the term is used especially when her partner is married. The relationship generally is stable and at least semi-permanent; however, the couple does not live together openly. In addition, the relationship is usually, but not always, secret. There is an implication that a mistress may be "kept"—i.e., that the lover is paying for some of the woman's living expenses.

Historically, the term has denoted a "kept woman", who was maintained in a comfortable (or even lavish) lifestyle by a wealthy man so that she will be available for his sexual pleasure. Such a woman could move between the roles of a mistress and a courtesan depending on her situation and environment. In modern times, however, the word "mistress" is used primarily to refer to the female lover of a man who is married to another woman in the case of an unmarried man, it is usual to speak of a "girlfriend" or "partner." Historically, a man "kept" a mistress. As the term implies, he was responsible for her debts and provided for her in much the same way as he did his wife, although not legally bound to do so. In more recent times, it is more likely that the mistress has a job of her own and is less, if at all, financially dependent on the man.

A mistress is not a prostitute. While a mistress, if "kept", may essentially be exchanging sex for money, the principal difference is that a mistress keeps herself exclusively reserved for one man, in much the same way as a wife and, there is not so much of a direct *quid pro quo* between the money and the sex act. There is usually an emotional and possibly social relationship between a man and his mistress, whereas the relationship to a prostitute is predominantly sexual. It is also important that the "kept" status follow the establishment of a relationship of indefinite term as opposed to the agreement on price and terms established prior to any activity with a prostitute.

The dangers of having a mistress are often overlooked because society seems to be more acceptable to certain behaviors primarily because a number of lawmakers are engaged in similar behaviors and if we stop one, a great deal of stoppage will need to commence because of the web many are entangled within. For a man who is married with a mistress, sadly she will more than likely never be more than the role he has given her or the role she has chosen to assume. Men are not exempt from being a mistress however; the proper term for a man who engages in a secretive relationship with a married woman is "Lover, Boy Toy, Gigolo, Back-door-Man or master.

Once a Typecast Always a Typecast

Some of the world's most talented actors understand what it means to be typecast. Many of them began their careers maybe as a child star and the world grew infatuated with them as a child star that it ultimately isolated them into a time capsule preventing growth from occurring. In most cases with men who have mistresses, many of them see her as an escape from the problems he encounters with his wife. She is an adventure or excitement from the boredom he is experiencing in his marriage. She could be a sex object. A good friend with exceptional benefits or someone he can grow old. The latter of that statement is a rarity, statistically only 3% of married men marry their affair partners and 3% of those actually work according to psychiatrists. Moreso, a study shows that of the men who end their marriages for their mistress, only 25% of those couples stayed together after marriage. The reason for this 75% rate is due in part to distrust of their partner, marriage in general, guilt or disappointment.

Our appetite will set in motion a series of decisions that are not necessarily beneficial to us long-term yet, it satisfies an immediate desire. A woman who begins her relationship as a mistress has a slight and slim chance of evolving from that role into a more lucrative position such as a fiancé or even a wife. The small percentage of those who actually become wives often have ongoing struggles because the man simply typecast her into primarily being his mistress, the secret Santa or the exciting thunderous Tuesday lunch date. Once the suspense and the aura of getting caught, which often times add an element of mystery to a relationship void of true substance subsides men and women are off to the next adventure to feed their appetite for the illustrious moments he/she experienced with the previous mate.

Escaping the Illusions

What I found interesting about affairs is that they are primarily built upon fantasy, deceit and at times guilt. The idea of engaging in a secretive affair with a woman who is not the wife lends to some type of movie plot that seems to always produce a happy ending and a pleasurable sexual experience driven by lust and lubricated by emotional romantic passion.

The phrase "The grass is greener on the other side", is frequently used to describe why men and women venture outside of their relationship to bond with someone else, but is the grass truly greener or is it just an illusion?

As I stated before those relationships are built on superficial and unrealistic expectations therefore, may not genuinely be better than your existing relationship.

When I was in my early twenties and had no expectation from what my life would become I partied, engaged in illicit meaningless relationships, and frivolously spent money as if I had an unlimited supply all because I was living for the moment and not looking beyond it. In 1996, I began to dabble with emceeing and finagled my way into a small club located on the southwest side of Atlanta, GA. This establishment was properly named "Club Escape". Club Escape was an exciting nightlife facility that allowed its patrons to escape from the stress and hectic moment's life presented during the workweek, into a blissful escapade of music, enticing liquor for men and women who hopelessly needed an entertaining venture to mentally flee from any thoughts of responsibility. The name was certainly befitting because we escaped weekly to this club and participated in a number of activities that seemed relevant at the moment. Yet, for me, it was after those moments when the soliloquy of the confidence building alcoholic beverages wore off that I realized my life was spiraling out of control.

Now if Club Escape was not enough for my budding eagerness, I eventually moved my weekend party a few miles down the street to a club that was bigger, better, and more out of control. This club had a number of things that Club Escape lacked from drinks to women and its name painted the picture for what its patrons would experience once entering its doors. This club was properly named "Illusions" and that is exactly what we received an illusion of reality. Club Illusions was filled to capacity every weekend and full of celebrities, neighborhood gangsters, and community leaders who all enjoyed a plethora of whatever their hearts desired. The problem with Club Illusions, like that of a spouse who engages in extramarital affairs, its owners and promoters were exceptional at creating a mirage of what was present. That mirage, for many of its partygoers after they spent all of their rent, food and, gas money to experience a good time for a few hours that they had to return to the reality of whatever life they dropped off at the security checkpoint before entering the club each week. The life they were eluding was not magically disappearing, it was patiently waiting on them to return and claim it at the end of the night much like those who eagerly dropped off their children to a babysitter prior to the club. At some point, the babysitter expects them to return to claim their possessions.

Those experiences allowed many to flee into an atmosphere that presented livable life sized upgrades that seemed to be far greater than the present reality awaiting them weekly.

The Growing Costs of Upgrades

Mobile advertisers and marketers have developed campaigns over the years that keep consumers upgrading their plans, phones or accessories because they understand our need for what we consider a better product.

Would you be surprised if I informed you that many of those advertisers are banking on enticing your primitive urge to sell their product faster every time!

I worked for an advertising firm in 1996 and one of the primary techniques they taught us was to sell potential customers on the following: Jones Effect, Fear of Loss and Rehash.

Jones Effect: "Keeping Up with the Joneses" is an idiom in many parts of the English-speaking world referring to the comparison to one's neighbor as a benchmark for social caste or the accumulation of material goods. To fail to "keep up with the Joneses" is perceived as demonstrating socio-economic or cultural inferiority. Because someone else is seemingly more efficient or compatible, many men and women tend to upgrade only to find the software is a bit more complicated than advertised, the car burns more gas than the one traded or, the computer has less memory or functions than the old one because they made room for the new features. Contrary to what the reasons are, upgrading because someone offers improved or has enhanced goods and services does not signify that what's advertised, offered or marketed is superior.

Fear of Loss: When you see something advertised and it says "won't last long or buy today" those are fear of loss statements that generally convince those interested in purchasing to do so in a timely manner or risk losing the item. Men and women fear if they do not engage or consent to an affair that they may lose a good candidate. Word to the wise, if they were that good the relationship would not have a need to be a secret nor require a hasty response. This tactic is utilized to cause you to make erratic decisions on impulse only to find those decisions costly after the adrenaline has subsided.

Rehash: When we rehashed consumers in the field, it consisted of us soliciting them to buy more of the same product. We did not change the product; we simply offered more of the same product but with a different tone. Many are being offered a new mate with the same or inferior issues the current mate possesses.

Regardless of what the item offered, with many upgrades comes stipulations and in the case of your wireless provider an added fee and extended contract.

17 LAYING IN HER LAP

Vulnerability is not divulging your secrets to someone who will expose himself or herself as well; it is freely giving access to your safe without a proper background check.

Laying in the lap of a woman brings a sense of comfort to a man. It allows him to be vulnerable because he feels safe and secure with her and he knows that as she strokes his tender head she is also stroking his fragile ego. The subtle touch she gives him massages the alienated soul that longs to pour out his heart in that very instance divulging his deepest and darkest secrets without prejudice or judgment. Laying his head in the lap of a woman who he is neither married nor committed could be risky. For him, trusting her to care for him in his weakest hour but for her, it could be an opportunity to take advantage of his vulnerability enabling her to manipulate him and coerce him into relinquishing the covenant which he has made with his wife.

For the woman who sincerely loves her man and cares for him as much as he cares for her a lap moment can be priceless because most men never trust their woman enough to disclose the cloak-and-dagger that may later haunt him upon being disclosed in an heated argument.

Delilah is the woman in the valley of Sorek whom Samson loved and who was his downfall. Motivated by greed, Delilah used her persistence to wear down Samson. His infatuation with her made Samson a venerable target. For all his physical strength, he was no match for her, and paid a great price for giving into her. A person's greatest accomplishment may well be helping others accomplish great things. Likewise, a person's greatest failure may be preventing others from achieving greatness.

Her Plan Is A Game: Strategic & Tactical

A game is structured playing, usually undertaken for enjoyment and sometimes used as an educational tool. Games are distinct from work, which is usually carried out for remuneration, and from art, which is more often an expression of aesthetic or ideological elements. When we itemize the games that are played in life the hustle game, the lying game, the manipulation game, the fake it to you make it game, the rich stealing from the poor game, the I love you but I want to be with someone else game and so forth, how does a man or woman who has been a victim of games avoid gamers?

I found a few basic principles utilized when a woman's plan is to manipulate a man for selfish gain. We must understand that her approach is not happenstance or dumb luck, her plan is strategic and tactical likened to that of a military strike.

When Delilah set her sights on Samson she saw him from miles away (not literally) but she possessed a determination that would not allow her to quit pursuing his secret until she gained it. Many who deceive and manipulate have what I call a backend reward awaiting, and for, Delilah as some women today her reward was financial.

When someone has a strategy, it is his or her plan of action designed to achieve a vision. The United States Military often creates strategies to pursue terrorist and war criminals or in some cases to rescue troops or everyday people from dangerous situations. Military strategy deals with the planning and conduct of campaigns, the movement and disposition of forces, and the deception of the enemy.

The father of modern strategic study, Carl von Clausewitz, defined military strategy as "the employment of battles to gain the end of war." B. H. Liddell Hart's definition put less emphasis on battles, defining strategy as "the art of distributing and applying military means to fulfill the ends of policy". Hence, both gave the pre-eminence to political aims over military goals.

If we do not inspect more of what we expect from relationships or people we intend on pursuing, dating or engaging in sexual relations, we can find ourselves like Samson on the brutal receiving end of a strategic plan with full tactical gear attached.

When someone is tactical, they are very skillful or diplomatic. This means they show cleverness and skill in tactics used to obtain something.

Game Plan: Alluring & Elusive

Delilah's game plans were alluring to Samson and contained illusive elements because he could not ascertain her objective although she had proven to be untrustworthy. In this sorrowful story of a man who is so blinded by lust and emotion that as her motives were revealed during each failed attempt to acquire the secrets to his strength, Samson could not decipher between ulterior motives and genuine concern and therefore, succumbed under pressure. Delilah's plan was alluring because it was captivating. She was able to entice Samson with what he needed, which was affection and adoration. Her plan was flawed because it involved an elusive nature that perpetuated the truth and deceived its target into believing that it actually cared about his well-being and wanted to sincerely help him.

Coaches across the globe in baseball, swimming, football and basketball all devise strategies to win games. Those schemes are meant to be duplicity because the opposing coach isn't suppose to determine the schemes beforehand therefore, eliminating any possibility of a counter strike. When we encounter those with alluring and elusive plans, we are not given the opportunity to counter attack with a plan that would expose the treachery allowing us to combat the game plan.

We must decide what type of relationship we want before emotions get involved, hence eradicating the possibility of allowing those emotions to cause us to make permanent decisions based upon temporary situations.

Understand that an elusive plan is meant to go undetected and its creator has the ability to lure you inward with tasty treats that feed your starving emotional, physical and mental needs but, lack the ability to feed your spirit.

How to identify Alluring and Elusive Plans:
- Pay attention to what is said
- Allow actions to speak louder than words
- Listen for what's not being said
- Identify motives before actions take form
- Inspect! Inspect! Inspect!

PART FOUR: HER TOUCH

⏻ Power Point to Ponder

Hidden needs will evolve when caressed and touched properly. You must carefully monitor who has access to those needs and when they are being neglected.

❓ Question to Consider

Are you carefully monitoring the hands on your heart? Are you constantly entrapped by your sweet tooth cravings? Will you continuously lie in the lap of strategic, tactical, alluring and elusive plans allowing them to go undetected?

💎 Jewel Tip

To become her "**BOAZ**" will require you to allow God to develop you into a man with sincerity, heart, character and integrity.

POWER NOTES:

PART FIVE

HER LOVE

THE GLASS HALF EMPTY 18

The relationships we build or break today could be the bridge to our destiny or ocean that floods any opportunities for advancement.

Have you ever witnessed a dog that is visibly thirsty drinking from a bowl that is inadequately filled? We have often heard the term the glass half empty is also half-full, but what does that saying actually mean and how does it apply to life and relationships? When I view this term I think of men who are half-empty in their relationships but have operated with a love canister filled with fluids that do not meet the daily quota necessary to for him to feel fulfilled, loved or appreciated.

Receiving part of anything is never as rewarding as receiving something in its entirety. Can you imagine working a forty or eighty hour workweek only to receive a portion of your paycheck? In the widely popular, book His Needs…Her Needs by Willard F. Hartley he states that we all have a love bank and if more withdrawals are made than deposits our love account will operate in the red with insufficient funds. When a man or woman operates at a deficit, the relationship is susceptible to a number of outside influences and opportunities. This truth is due in part because men and women have varying needs and those needs are often predicated on their mate providing for those needs consistently. Relationships suffer when men and women fail to adequately research what all is needed for their mate to feel sufficient. We invest in a number of things from stock options and retirement funds to houses and stylish wardrobes. How many of us actually take those identical approaches and invest in our relationships? How many men and women are suffering from relational starvation? Studies show that women often begin to entertain the possibility of an affair not because she is curious and wants sex from another man yet; it is due in part to her lack of attention at home. The man somehow has faltered in providing security, affection or companionship and someone else has shown an interest in those things that her spouse seems to overlook or take for granted.

Accepting a Fraction of Love

A profoundly tender, passionate affection for another person is one of the definitions of *LOVE*. Love is an emotion of strong affection and personal attachment. It is a virtue representing all of human kindness, compassion and affection and, the unselfish loyal benevolent concern for the good of another. If love was, an inheritance left to you by your royal father, would you accept just a fraction of it or, would you want the entire inheritance.

Men and women across the globe are settling for a fraction of love out of fear that the love bank is somehow drying up and rather than risk the chance of receiving no love at all, they will settle for a meager portion of what they truly desire. Is that a way to live? How many of us share this story? Regardless if this is your situation today or was yours a few years ago, I believe that a price was paid for love and many of us often give ours away to the wrong people as Samson did with Delilah. This costly mistake places us in a venerable position of repetitive manipulation because our good-natured heart longs to feel the love we often disperse yet; it will also deceive us to believe that receiving a portion of love is just as good as receiving all of love.

Glad You Love Me At All

I was watching the romantic comedy film, Hitch starring Will Smith as professional "date doctor" Alex Hitchens who makes a living teaching men how to woo women. In one scene, Smith's character has a flashback moment to how he became a matchmaker. It shows him arm in arm with his college girlfriend, who is not feeling as attached to him as he is to her. Hitchens looks her in her eyes and says, "You don't have to be in love with me, I'm just glad you love me at all". I said to myself what happened to him in his short life that taught him to settle.

I often say to my empowerment clients "go after what you want or, you could spend your entire life settling for what you can get". I am personally not a settler and therefore, would never settle for a fraction of someone's love or be excited by the fact that they love me just a little.

How true is my above statement? I would be a liar if I told you that the confidence that I may display today always existed. Truth of the matter is I can personally identify with wanting love so badly that any type of attention being displayed would constitute to me that it was love although it was merely a fragment of my imagination. I shared in an earlier chapter that my father wasn't around much when I was growing up, but what I didn't share with you was how that affected my love bank and how I spent a great deal of my life searching for his love in most of my relationships.

Searching for Samson

How could I ever become the strong, loving, caring and affectionate man like Samson when my heart possessed gaping holes that you could drive an eighteen-wheeler through? The void created by not having the man I thought would teach me about the birds and the bees, play catch with me on Saturday mornings or, be a voice at PTA meetings was more detrimental than I imagined. I was a bit ascetic when it came to dating I never felt like I was a good catch or offered much to women. My journey begins in my neighborhood with a few of my friends who were older men and had a great deal of experience under their belts and wisdom in their beards. The men were teenagers but to me they were father figures because they seemed to know so much about women and how to treat them. I often would seek them out just to hear their dialogue and take mental notes. In 2006, while visiting a media convention in Jacksonville, FL I was told that I had a mind like a file cabinet therefore, I tend to store information for future use and that is exactly what I began to do with the group of teenagers I would hang around.

Samson's strength was God given for the task he was slated to accomplish yet, his weakness was he was controlled by sensuality. As I read his story I often asked myself, what was he missing that kept him seemingly searching? Was Samson's void of love and affection from his parents? Did he somehow feel alienated by his superhuman assignment? Or, was he like a number of us who hide behind the shell of our gifts, high positions at work, clergy calling, money, or social status while screaming for an ear to listen to the brokenness of solitude reverberating from within our souls because we weren't given enough hugs as children.

I have learned as I have grown that my search was for acceptance. I felt as if my father did not want me and I longed for his acceptance and because I did not receive it from him, I sought it in my peers and when they didn't grant it, my search continued in the women I dated. This cycle continued for years and at times now I find myself searching for it in the still of the night when the applauds from the crowd of empowering chanters have withdrawn to a silent hush and I feel inadequate.

Your question may be the same one I had years ago and in your quest to discover the answer, you will begin your search for Samson. I believe we must identify, dissect, operate and heal in order to unearth our inner Samson.

Identify the Problem: We must ascertain our issues if we are to rectify them.

Dissect the Findings: Breaking down the issues into categories will better assist us in solidifying the proper remedy necessary, tools needed and, procedure to follow.

Operate: Serious injuries according to doctors require an operation to repair the damaged components. If we do not cut out the wounded areas, growth will not commence.

Allow Time to Heal: After an operation we must allow the proper time to heal and while healing, receive the proper nourishment necessary to insure a total recovery. Patience will become your friend during this process. Leaving the hospital too soon may result in further damage to your wounds.

19 WHAT THE WIFE REFUSES THE GIRLFRIEND WON'T

What we give up today to get what we desire may prove to be more costly tomorrow when the taxes are due.

All men have heard the dreadful statement "Once you get married sex stops". That statement has haunted married men for generations and continues to be the ongoing joke at bachelor parties across the country. Truth is hardly anything that you experienced in the dating and courting phase carries over to the marriage after a while. You must continuously work on implementing or maintaining those intricate moments that you consider vital to the growth and development of your relationship. Marriage is only difficult when we cease to satisfy our mate unselfishly versus our own selfish needs.

Most couples fail at building a healthy marriage because many lose focus of their marital purpose. *Ephesians 5:25* requires husbands to love their wives as Christ loved the church, and that passage of scripture does not suggest that only happens if she does something in return. A few scriptures before that one in *Ephesians 5:22* Wives, submit to your husband's as to the Lord. I would think if we are following the word as born again believers or Christians, why do so many God lovers and followers end up in divorce court?

That could be an ongoing question with an assortment of replies but I found an interesting scripture that many may forget exist. Proverbs 5:19 says, *"She is a loving deer, a graceful doe. Let her breasts satisfy you always. May you always be captivated by her love" (New Living Translation).* If the wife is to satisfy the husband for the duration of the marriage why are so many men venturing out into shark infested territory seeking satisfaction?...the answer is many feel that their wives are refusing to care for them and therefore as the saying goes "What you won't do, someone else will".

When men and women engage in either emotional or physical relationships there are varying needs by both parties that must be fulfilled in order for tranquility to subsist. Relationships without a give and give margin (*a relationship where both parties are giving versus a give and take relationship*) may be susceptible to outside influences, which may wedge gaps between husband and wife causing either to seek marital counsel elsewhere.

Rejections Lead To Erections

It has happened to all of us: an office proposal is rejected, a demo tape is returned, slides are sent back with a form letter, or a pitch meets a stony reception. You are devastated of course, and may contemplate hanging up your apron and calling it quits. Whether it is your first or fiftieth rejection does not seem to make it any easier.

There are ways of coping with rejection that can speed you through some of the bumpier parts.

Like the stages of grief, these steps are not always done in order and you might need to go back to one or more before you are complete. That is okay; just like art, it is the journey that counts more than the destination.

Rejection may come from many sources and those sources can be viewed as ridiculous for some but extremely serious for others. Incidentally, the most common reason for rejection is a feeling of inadequacy and a fear of failure from your partner.

Men are designed to love women and make love to them as well. When a woman denies her man of the intimacy that was programmed in his DNA by God it creates a dilemma and ultimately leads him to seek fulfillment with other women. I am not suggesting that his decision to forsake his marital vows and commitment to care for his wife is acceptable. I am merely stating the obvious and my rationale is not present in all marital cases but many. Researchers suggest that the internet, email, chat rooms and social media networks are making it easier for people to engage in infidelity. When a wife rejects her husband it can cause him to feel unwanted by her and therefore, he begins to entertain the flattering advances by his co-worker, business manager or casual gym member.

I once read a story of a couple who was devastated by an affair or in this case, many affairs that the husband carried out. He says his yielding to the ongoing temptation in his relationship was due in part to the deterioration of intimate moments him and his wife shared. Those moments became far and between as their relationship progressed. He found himself alone most weeks because of his wife's travel schedule and when she was home she did not particularly want to be bothered with intimacy or sex. The man stated that he found other ways to entertain himself for a while and because of his religious beliefs, did not engage in self-pleasure but his raging hormones were only getting more intense and he knew if the denial persisted that he would fold eventually.

The game changer for him came when he approached his wife after one of her long road trips and suggested that they get away for the weekend before her next trip and enjoy one another as they once did earlier in their marriage. The wife refused citing how tired she was. The husband went out to get dinner but upon his return discovered, that his wife was pleasuring herself in the tub and seemingly having thoughts of someone else as she passionately moaned the name of another man while climaxing. He felt if someone enthralled his wife that maybe she had lost interest in him sexually and those advances that he received daily now seemed delightful.

The advances that he once fought off were now enticing him and eventually led to an affair. The other woman provided adventures that his wife did not. She listened when his wife argued, she allowed him to introduce new sexual experiences that his wife shunned, and she gave him support in all of his endeavors not just the ones she shared a mutual interest.

The girlfriend (AKA the other woman) is seemingly able and willing to provide what he is refused at home and that allowed for an illustrious exotic and erotic escapade.

The Catcher In the Rye

Although I believe we have choices no matter what situations we are faced with at home, the man's wife did not help her husband with his growing desires when she rejected her Godly obligations to satisfy him with her love and affection.

Many couples across the country are experiencing a lack of intimacy and researchers suggest that this drop in productivity occurs at various moments during relationships. While infidelity can occur at anytime in a relationship, there are certain times when it is more likely to occur than others are. In addition, there are certain relationship factors, which can dramatically increase the potential for infidelity.

Throughout the life of nearly all relationships, four timetable events can breed infidelity.

After the First Year of Marriage. This is generally a time at which most people would not consider the likelihood of infidelity to be that great. For this reason, it is also the time when affairs are the least detected.

After the first year of marriage, the honeymoon ends, and the representative begins to set in. The emotional high that both partners experienced during the wedding is gone. This leaves a void. It is similar to the effects of drugs. Once you are high and come back down, you want to get high again. The new husband or wife may no longer consistently supply what is needed to find that high.

Affairs occurring after the first year of marriage are almost never detected, and are typically just flings. There is no real emotional attachment to the other person and the cheating partner can still feel love with their new husband or wife. Regardless if it happens here, the chances of it happening again later on in the relationship have increased substantially.

After the First Child is Born. This occurrence can sometimes be blended in with the previous scenario, as many couples may have their first child after the first year of marriage. Aside from that, the reasons between the two can be very different.

Children change a relationship no matter how you look at it. Moreover, the first child is always more traumatic than the rest. It brings about stress, fatigue and, the need to give the majority of your attention to someone other than your husband or wife. While affairs after the first year of marriage are brought about by an individual's feelings towards himself or herself, affairs after the first child are brought on by the couple's feelings towards each other.

The 5th to 7th Year. This is widely referred to as the seven-year itch. It does not imply that at exactly the seven-year point in a marriage, someone will have an affair. What it does mean is that somewhere around this time, it may occur. This is due to the relationship running its natural course and achieving the goals which had been set. For instance, a couple gets married, has kids, buys their dream house and establishes their careers. So what's left now? Doing the same thing day in and day out for the rest of their lives? Growing old and bored together? The anticipation of greater things to come is gone.

This scenario is the most common cause of all affairs. A man or woman may feel that the "project is completed" and nothing is left to do but sit and watch the days pass. They are bored, unhappy or just plain tired of living the American dream. A new house may be purchased, perhaps a new car or having another baby. Anything to add some excitement. But the rush from these quick fixes is short-lived and bittersweet at best.

Affairs occurring at this stage in the relationship are often the most damaging. The cheating individual traditionally develops a deep bond with the other person. The faithful mate will question the others fidelity more than at any other point. Affairs occurring during this period will continue for the longest period as well.

Middle Age. Also known as the mid-life crisis. This is where the children are all grown and have left an empty nest. At this point, both men and women begin to question their lot in life. They are essentially back where they started; a couple living together with no children to care for. Except now, they have around twenty years of experience with each other. This lends itself to the question of whether they want to spend another twenty plus years with the same individual.

This second childhood so to speak brings around noticeable changes in both mates. A man might buy a sports car; a woman might feel the need for a new youthful hairstyle. Both may start exercising or purchase a new, "younger" wardrobe. Whatever the particulars, they will not do this for the benefit of the other. They will be doing it for themselves as much as for anyone other than their mate.

In spite of your situation at home, you must make a decision to honor your marital vows and your mate. We have all made mistakes and wrong choices in life and will more than likely continue to do so without becoming rooted in God's word but the great news is that God is forgiving and will provide opportunities of restoration and redemption. We must fight the temptation to look outside our marriages with God's word and a sturdy application of prayer, fasting, consistent communication with your spouse, status updates and activities together that promote healthy relationships.

If we never open the window to adultery, we will never walk in the door of infidelity. Today make a choice to be honorable!

WHAT'S MISSING? 20

A locked door is just a door without a key to open it. A kitchen is just a room with cluttered utensils and over exposed poultry without a chef to tame its content and manage its inventory.

Have you ever cooked a meal and upon tasting it felt like it was good but something was missing? Have you packed to go on a trip and went over your check list but your gut instinct said to you that you may have left something out of your suitcase? At times, everyone has encountered a bout with feeling incomplete. I remember going through the entire year of fourth grade only to get an incomplete from my teacher and retained. In that moment, I realized that although I may have demonstrated a great deal of progress my teacher felt something was missing that would not allow me to be successful at the next grade level. The startling discovery of life's journey is that we can accomplish a great deal of goals and objectives yet seem unfulfilled with where we are or what we are doing. Many of us may have answers to a number of questions in the classroom at school, in the boardroom at work or in the bedroom at home but somehow when we are on the balcony of our voyage alone we simply can't answer the question of "What's Missing?"

As men we may have the house, the car, we have entertained many lovely young women, given various promotions and advancement in our careers and still do not have a sense of accomplishment.

Many of us journey through life with void like feelings thirsting for fulfillment and will search through a number of empty canisters in despair neglecting to find what we were seeking. What do you do when money does not quench your appetite? What do you invest in when the growing portfolio of stocks and bonds whither with unfulfilled expectations? What happens to your cravings when no sexual encounter seems to have the fire to satisfy your erotic feelings of separation? All of these are exceptional questions yet I believe there are several answers.

Identifying what we need to feel fulfilled in life is a quest by itself and many never truly begin the search and therefore, find themselves on an adventure that seems to continue like an unsolved mystery.

Cold Case Files

Cold Case is an American police procedural television series, which ran on CBS from 2003 to 2010. The series revolved around a fictionalized Philadelphia Police Department division that specializes in investigating cold cases. The show is set in Philadelphia, Pennsylvania and follows Detective Lilly Rush (Kathryn Morris), a homicide detective with the Philadelphia Police Department, who specializes in "cold cases", or investigations which are no longer being actively pursued by the department.

Have you ever considered that maybe you're running bland on your color of love because you feel like your relationships end up cold cases? What is missing from you and your relationship could be your unfulfilled fantasy fixation of some imaginative desire that is ailing you secretly.

We often see other women who we admire from afar because they seem to possess something that we desire inwardly and something that we hope they can give us but the reality is the fantasy is unfounded because you may never find out unless you make a choice to engage.

I asked a friend of mine who was married fifteen years, yet in the middle of a divorce at what point did he notice a change and if he identified what the change was. For many of us changes begin to occur early in the relationship and we may fail to see those changes or choose to ignore them for fear of what may happen if we address them.

What we are searching for is a void from within and we must identify the cause of that void or we may continue to suffer from its effects. **James 1:14** says, *"Temptation comes from our own desires, which entice us and drag us away."* In addition, verse 15 further states *"Then, after desire has conceived, it gives birth to sin; and sin, when it is full-grown, gives birth to death."* What a powerful scripture!!!! This scripture allows us to see the pattern of how our thoughts create actions and how those actions when fully developed breed sin and once sin has entered our being it births death. This death is not necessarily a physical one but it creates a separation from our heavenly father and once we are entangled without repentance we attempt to fill those voids with more sin or wrongdoing.

What is missing is the power that we gain from communing with God and the strength he grants us to fight and defeat ANY temptation that we are faced with. I often share with people that when the bible says in Genesis 1:27, *"So God created man in his own image, in the image of God he created him; male and female he created them."*

God is spirit and if we study his very being we understand that we are spirit wrapped up in flesh and embodying a soul, therefore how we remain in Christ Jesus is by filling our hearts with his word.

John 1:1 eloquently states what I am suggesting, *"In the beginning was the Word, and the Word was with God, and the Word was God."* If the word was in the beginning and it was indeed God, then the more we fill our hearts with the word the more we become Christ like and therefore are not subject to the laws of sin or our sinful nature outside of God and his word.

We can only fill what is missing in the word of God the bible says that the word is quick and sharper than a double edge sword hence, it answers fast and cuts quick. Allow God to construct those missing pieces filling you with prosperity and hope forming you into the man who loves from within because he has no areas of emptiness pushing him to seek satisfaction in dark alleys of lustful palaces.

21 MATTERS OF THE HEART

The heart is deceitful above all things, and desperately wicked: who can know it? I the LORD search the heart, I try the reins, even to give every man according to his ways, and according to the fruit of his doings. Jeremiah 17:9-10

Would you believe me if I told you that what we say reveals what is in our hearts? Jesus seems to remind us of this fact in Matthew 12:34-36 *"You brood of snakes! How could evil men like you speak what is good and right? For whatever is in your heart determines what you say. A good person produces good things from the treasury of a good heart, and an evil person produces evil things from the treasury of an evil heart. And I tell you this, you must give an account on judgment day for every idle word you speak. The words you say will either acquit you or condemn you."* What types of words come out of your mouth? Many people are led by their hearts, which is said to be wicked and deceiving according to scripture. I have journeyed on the roller coaster of heartfelt decisions only to find disappointment, frustration and bitterness.

Luke 6:45 *"A good man out of the good treasure of his heart bringeth forth that which is good; and an evil man out of the evil treasure of his heart bringeth forth that which is evil: for of the abundance of the heart his mouth speaketh."*

The heart is tricky because it will cause us to make irrational decisions, act without thinking, and deceive us greatly as it relates to us exercising true discernment in relationships.

I know too well, how the heart can lead you into lovable pastures only to slaughter you while grazing. Women always classified me as a "Good Man" and that often placed my heart in a position that seemed venerable to me. Women would mistreat me and most times cheat on me with men who were a bit more rugged and harsh. My mother taught me how to love women as I loved her and therefore I figured that was the proper way to treat women. As I have gotten older I realized, it wasn't how I treated them that allowed them to misuse me, it was those women not understanding what a Jewel Expert could do for them long-term.

We must understand that what is in our heart we will demonstrate by our actions and what we say. If love resides in you, then the things you display will resemble true love and if malice and deceit is in you those things will take shape and protrude out of you as well.

Change of Heart

Change of Heart was a television dating show that aired from 1998-2003. The premise of the show involved dating couples who are matched with other singles and sent out on respective dates. During the taping, they discuss their relationship, then their new dating experience. At the end of the show the couples must decide if they want to Stay Together, or if they've had a Change Of Heart.

As fascinating as the show was, it allowed couples to witness the identity of their hearts. Many fought to stay together while others experienced embarrassment as their mate decided that life would be better without them. We have decisions we must make daily concerning our lives and those decisions often will include matters concerning our heart. We often wonder how we can experience a breakup or setback in life and feel as though we have healed but as soon as we encounter our ex-boyfriend or girlfriend or another setback we feel all of the emotions from the previous event.

King Saul once consulted a medium for direction and guidance after God would not answer him during his time of need. Saul had recently banished mediums and psychics from Israel to rid it of witchcraft however, in desperation he deceived and sought a medium to call up the spirit of the prophet Samuel in order to hear from God.

Although Saul had removed the sin of witchcraft from the land, he did not remove it from his heart. We may make a great show of denouncing sin, but if our hearts do not change, the sins will return. Knowing what is right and condemning what is wrong does not take the place of doing what is right.

Our change of heart must come from our deliverance and not our outward show of manipulation.

Time for a Heart Transplant

A heart transplant, or a cardiac transplantation, is a surgical transplant procedure performed on patients with end-stage heart failure or severe coronary artery disease. As of 2007, the most common procedure was to take a working heart from a recently deceased organ donor (cadaveric allograft) and implant it into the patient. The patient's own heart is either removed (orthotropic) or, less commonly, left in place to support the donor heart (heterotypic); both were controversial solutions to an enduring human ailment.

Many of us are silently suffering from heart failure refusing to acquire the proper procedure necessary to correct the issue. In order for us to experience the peace that God offers and be able to forgive and forget, (many say they will forgive but they will not forget...News Flash that is not forgiveness). Even God forgets hence the scripture in Isaiah 43:25, *"I, even I, am he who blots out your transgressions, for my own sake, and remembers your sins no more.* Our hearts should be soft, pliable, trusting and open to change. Ezekiel 11:19-21 says *"I will give them an undivided heart and put a new spirit in them; I will remove from them their heart of stone and give them a heart of flesh. Then they will follow my decrees and be careful to keep my laws. They will be my people, and I will be their God. But as for those whose hearts are devoted to their vile images and detestable idols, I will bring down on their own heads what they have done, declares the Sovereign Lord."*

In order to be restored both physically and spiritually we must receive a new heart from God and receive his spirit within us to transform and be empowered to do his will. No matter how impure your life is at the moment or the mistakes you have made in the past, God offers you a fresh start. You can have your sins washed away, receive a new heart from God and have his spirit within you. This will allow you to heal properly and truly experience the love a woman has for you without manipulation, deceit or intentional heartbreak.

NO LOVE GIVEN
NO LOVE TO GIVE   22

You can never give what you do not possess!

How difficult would it be to acquire water from a well that is dry? I suppose impossible, I would further say that retrieving something from anything that is barren is virtually impractical. A close friend of mine spent most of her life in foster care and found that her interactions with people who seemingly were present one moment only to be removed the next were superficial. She realized that the absence of care in her life from those that she cared for rendered her emotionless and at times seemed very cold and uncaring to those she encountered. Her journey to find freedom spun her on a whirlwind of encounters that at times paralyzed her emotionally and caused severe damage to her love fountain.

Those experiences made her feel as if her internal town had been hit with a tsunami that washed everything she possessed inwardly to shore and did not include a return to sender stamp. This story beckoned me to ask the question "How can someone give something outwardly that they don't have internally". Thelma felt as if she could never give love when she herself never felt love from those she reverenced.

This is a common problem in many communities, and often goes undetected and therefore cannot be rectified. A repetition of hurt, disappointment or any type of trauma can cause us to be withdrawn from giving because we may feel as though so much has been taken away from us.

I lost my mother in April of 2000, my first marriage was in turmoil and we were going through a traumatic divorce, my uncle dies of a brain hemorrhage the following year, I was homeless and my grandmother passed away in February 2003, those events happening one after the other took so much from me that I literally felt motionless. As I reflect on those times, I am reminded of incidents that occurred long before those in my life. I believe my love tank began to leak during my first year of college and that journey is what ultimately set a few things in my life in motion and caused me to operate on fumes of love versus experiencing the true essence of love.

Heartbreak Hotel

I found what I believed to be my true love during my final two years of high school. She was a maverick; she stood alone in the crowded pond of beautiful swans. Her smile could light up a Broadway production radiant and inviting, her warm and meek spirit invited me to pursue her like a wild animal in the conga jungle and the way she carried herself assured me that she was a woman I wanted on my arm. I vigorously pursued her for months but was unsuccessful, talk about heartbreak hotel! My approach I thought was too aggressive and therefore, decided to relax and allow our paths to meticulously cross at the right time. That time was on a track trip to the University of Florida, when everything seemed to be going right. We somehow came together and were inseparable thereafter. We would go on to date throughout high school and into college. The magic bond that we created appeared unbreakable but then again we were seventeen years old so what could we possibly know about long-term commitment right! I believed that this woman was my soul mate and that we would be together forever. I attended a small junior college two hours away from Atlanta, GA while she attended an HBCU in Raleigh, NC, we both felt strong initially and then I begin to notice changes. I noticed our weekly phone conversations begin to lessen; she seemed a bit detached and even hinted at possibly dating other men.

I've always been an ambitious man, going after the things I desire so I never had to settle for what I could get, but this relationship seemed to be out of my power and I wasn't sure if I could save it with my determination and will to love. While on a school visit to North Carolina I stopped by to see my girlfriend and we spent a wonderful evening loving and enjoying each other's company until...

The Big Decision

Lebron James made headlines in 2009 when he held a huge press conference announcing that he would take his talents from the faithful followers of Cleveland, Ohio to South Beach. The day that my girlfriend revealed to me that she was involved with another man and was interested in continuing that relationship, I felt like the fans of the Cleveland Cavaliers, betrayed and heartbroken. The woman I believed I would spend the rest of my life with was no longer interested in playing on team Mo; the hurt I felt devastated me greatly and it was unfamiliar territory. It seemed very personal to me and at that moment, something happened to me that changed my life forever.

I bottled up those feelings of rejection, hurt and devastation so deep that deep sea divers could pull it up. I vowed that no one would ever hurt me like that again. I became an Ambassador for the

No Love campaign and to me no one was safe in my path. My disregard for women after that ordeal was very different from what my mother taught me growing up. I was so numb to pain that nothing affected me anymore and I remained so until I was in my late twenties.

The Big decision has an echo affect and trickled down my stony heart and into my livid soul. I just could not understand why she wasn't happy at home with me...

Why She Isn't Happy at Home

The moment she waited for her entire life is hours away. She has dreamed of walking down the aisle a dozen times, envisioning herself feeling like the queen her mother repeatedly uttered in her ear that she was when she was a little girl. She often wonders if this dream will ever end until the day, it actually does and then she wonders when she will be happy again. The fulfillment she encountered on her wedding day is refreshing and warranted. It is compared to someone receiving a miracle transplant or a family receiving a needed vacation in The Hamptons with Sean Combs and Donald Trump. Many would question if her delighted demeanor on her special day is authentic. What has transpired to cause her unhappiness at home? I am not sure if the remedy is available or exists. After my title bout with love landed me in intensive care and rendered me loveless for years, I decided to give love and trust a try again.

In 1996, I met a record producer who signed me to a label deal and we begin to build what seemed to be a great fit musically. I spent years learning and following many friends who were industry veterans to gain access to this lucrative industry that allowed thousands of artists to live their dream and funneled millions of records to adoring fans worldwide, however my deal went south and left me pondering about my future. While in search of a new journey, I met an amazing woman who immediately grabbed my attention and my heart. She was beautiful, intelligent sexy and sassy just my type I figured. We had remarkable chemistry and would talk for hours. We began a courtship that quickly turned into a full-blown relationship. This relationship was almost impossible to believe, it seemed that someone had taken a packet of instant family, poured it into a glass and stirred and just like that me, her and her two-year-old son was a happy family.

The journey was short-lived, my decision to relocate with my job was suppose to be a blessing for us however, it seemed to be the wedge that drove us apart. I began to morph back into the young man in college who bottled up his emotions and feelings and became reserved because my woman was becoming more ascetic each day. Before I left to move to North Carolina, my wonderful woman disclosed to me that she was expecting and that I would be a father soon. What a joy for us I thought, things quickly began to spiral downward as she was finding more excuses as to why she had not joined me in North Carolina as we discussed prior to my relocation. My visits to Atlanta seemed to go from every weekend to twice a month and then once a month as she was becoming increasingly busy with work. The nail in the coffin would come shortly after her holiday visit to Denver, CO revealed she was not happy at home with me.

When It Rains...The Bottom Falls Out

I would have used the subtitle, "When it rains it pours", but a simple pour would be an understatement in this case. On one of my weekend visits, I noticed that things were different with us, she was very withdrawn and I could not understand why. A few months prior, she disclosed that an ailment was discovered upon a routine visit to the doctor and that it would require surgery. That moment placed us in a precarious situation as we had to decide if we wanted to be parents or if I wanted to possible be a single father because the possibility of her not surviving if she did not have the surgery yet opt to have the baby were very slim.

My protective nature wanted to be there for her in this crucial and delicate time of our lives however, she suggested that I did not travel but tend to work during her surgery. I thought her request was rather odd and felt how could I allow the woman I loved to go through a possibly detrimental procedure and I stay at home in another state on the couch watching football all day. I packed a bag and after work drove the four hours to Atlanta making my destination in three hours, she was out of surgery and at her parents' home resting when I arrived so I drove to my mother's for the night. The next morning I awoke and phoned her but received no answer, I am literally perplexed at why the woman I love and figured loved me just as much was seemingly avoiding my calls all day. I finally drove the distance to her job…Oh yes she was back at work! My mother discerned that something was wrong and inquired, when I explained to her the situation she knew right away what the real issue was and alerted me that my woman had an abortion and not a medical procedure that she previous shared with me. My mother was a former nurse and understood the medical terms that I was oblivious to.

That fateful day I felt like the sky opened up and God allowed the rain to commence on my life as if he had on the earth centuries before when he flooded the earth for forty days and forty nights. This ordeal caused me to revisit my previous hurt only this time my reform was ten times worse. I learned over the years that when our love tank is empty we are reduced to providing fumes of what use to reside in us. We find ourselves dispensing fragile feelings of *extreme like* because we feel as though we have not received any love and therefore, we have no love to give.

It is difficult to pull from an empty source to fulfill the needs of others when we are lacking the proper nutrients to sustain a healthy relationship ourselves. Love is fragile when in the hands of irresponsible people and we must monitor our disposal of love to those we wish to date or marry because if we are not careful we could find ourselves on a roller coaster of adventure with a heart as cold as the great state of Alaska.

Love Deficient

Two of the most difficult sins to resist are pride and sexual immorality. Both are seductive. Pride says "I Deserve It" sexual desire says "I Need It". In combination, their appeal is deadly. Why is it that men and women find themselves entangled in sexual sins or adulterous acts? The bible suggests that pride and sexual enticement are the causes. When someone is deficient of something, it means they do not have enough of what is needed to sustain a healthy balance and therefore will lack one while in the need of another.

I have learned that you cannot sell something that you do not own. Many of you reading this book feel a deficiency when it comes to love. You either did not receive a great deal of it from those you gave it to or you have been hurt and damage to a degree that you have closed up your love doors from receiving or dispensing any love at all.

When we are deficient of love, we may often replace it with sex because it feels like love. Sexual enticement appeals to an empty heart just as pride appeals to an empty head.

What we must do to combat these two deadly sins is fill our head with God's wisdom while filling our hearts with his love. Something depleted must be refilled with substance or it may operate deficient on fumes disguised as authentic fuel.

LOVE JONES 23

If loving you is wrong, I relinquish the desire to be right, but if it is right to render love to you then I savory every moment to do so.

Love Jones is a 1997 American romantic drama film written and directed by Theodore Witcher, in his feature film debut. It stars Larenz Tate and Nia Long. Isaiah Washington, Bill Bellamy, and Lisa Nicole Carson lead the supporting cast. It is considered a classic work in African-American cinema.

"What do you do after love at first sight?" That's the question posed in this story set in Chicago. The independent film puts a modern spin on Modern Romance portraying two "confused lovebirds" that learn not to underestimate the powers of *"a Love Jones"*. The story calls to question the powers of attraction and fate, as well as the possibilities of love at first sight. Moreover, it questions the roles of romance and love in contemporary society.

In Chicago, Darius Lovehall (Larenz Tate) is a poet who is giving a reading at the Sanctuary, an upscale nightclub presenting jazz and poetry to a bohemian clientele. Shortly before his set, he meets Nina Mosley (Nia Long), a gifted photographer who recently lost her job. They exchange small talk, and Darius makes his interest clear when he renames his love poem "A Blues For Nina". A mutual attraction is sparked between them, and Darius invites himself back to her place to persistently ask her out. They have sex on the first date, but neither Darius nor Nina is sure where to go next after this promising start. Nina has just gotten out of a relationship and isn't sure if she still cares for her old boyfriend or not, while at the same time Darius' friends read him the riot act for wanting to give up his freedom so early on in the game. From then on, their relation and everything else change for both of them.

I absolutely love this movie, primarily because the storyline is so familiar to many of us and the characters in the film draw viewers into the plot and instantaneously give an electrifying aura of true love being discovered. Darius reminds me of a number of men I've had the pleasure of meeting over the years; he has an immediate attraction to Nina and after learning more about her is certain that they are meant to be together, yet his ego allows him to let her go. Darius has an opportunity to express his true feelings about Nina visiting her ex-boyfriend in New York but decides to go the macho route as if he was not affected by her desire to test the waters of romance and see if any ripples of amorous residue remained for her former beau.

Sex Ain't Better Than Love

R&B songster Trey Songz released an EP album entitled "Inevitable" which included the hit song "Sex Ain't Better Than Love", where he depicts an adventure that teaches him a few things about love that sex failed to demonstrate during his dance with the two of them. Many men when they feel the *"Jones"* of love often revert to what street corner philosophers or unknowing neighborhood teachers taught them about relationships however, those classes must have been fast tracked with outdated materials and supplies. The myth that sex cures all things in relationships is farfetched and inaccurate. You can have exhilarating sex present but have a host of tangibles absent from your relationship or have marginal tangibles and defunct sex present in your relationship either combination should not be a deciding factor in if you have a healthy or failing relationship.

Failing to invest in the corporeal aspects of your relationship (i.e., the moments spent together laughing at seemingly corny jokes, quality time loving the pure essence of each other, or the building process to a wonderful growing relationship) will prevent you from enjoying the silent love the two of you share. Men have spent thousands of dollars splurging on providing what they deem to be the finer things in life for their woman but often falling short in providing her with a sense of security and protection, affection, adoration or confident assurance that they're committed to growing and learning and learning and growing in the relationship.

Sex is definitely not better than enjoying the essence of loving someone regardless of their physical make up or romantic abilities. Darius and Nina taught us that having the "Love Jones" is what our community was built on and should remain a symbol of who we hope our children will grow to become. We can rest knowing that if we invest properly we will reap a just reward.

Love vs. Lust

Love and lust are very different. What appears to be love can quickly turn into hate therefore, proving the theory of love. Many will claim to be in love with someone when in fact they are actually overcome with lust. Love is patient; lust requires immediate satisfaction. Love is kind, lust is harsh. Love does not demand its own way, lust does. Lust may feel like love in the beginning but when physically expressed, it results in self-disgust and hatred of the other person. If patience is an issue for you, what you are feeling is not true love. Read **1Corinthians 13** for the characteristics of love.

Tough Love

Tough love is an expression used when one person treats another harshly or sternly with the intent to help them in the end. The phrase was evidently coined by Bill Milliken when he wrote the book *Tough Love* in 1968 and has been used by numerous authors since then.

The VH1 series entitled "Tough Love", where the host offers relationship advice for singles and couples. The show allowed men and women to journey for several weeks through a course of discovery and in doing so, presented a number of challenges and issues that prohibited them from achieving oneness in their relationships. The host then would do what many of us may need; he distributed an equal amount of tough love. He gave the participants advice and counsel that at times seemed hard but meaningful. Maybe you have enjoyed the undemanding comforts of self-indulged prophecy filling your mind with accolades of who you desire to be but having yet to become. Tough Love truth is that we all have areas that need improving and enhancements. How you love God and yourself will ultimately determine your ability to love others. It is time you start the race so in your running at some point you can cross the finish line ahead of the pack raising your hand in victory!

Learning to Love Again

When I broke my fibula and tibia it was a painful and at times frustrating journey to recovery but it was necessary to endure the anguish if I wanted to walk again. In life when we are hit with various traumatic experiences, we must press forward in order to love again. This love could be romantic, spiritual or in a friendship. Love is somewhat like trust when it pertains to people, it must be earned and once it has been dispensed, it is very difficult to get back without rehabilitation type training. Loving yourself is the key to allowing anyone else to love you or yourself to relinquish love to anyone else. Learning to love again will take patience; follow through, drive and determination. Allot room for smaller steps to lead to bigger leaps and you will find that it is easier to love again once you understand who is giving the love and who is in line to receive it.

THRILL OF VICTORY

24

Crossing the threshold of a completed race in front of the crowd breeds an exhilarating feeling known to many as the Thrill of Victory.

In 1988 the Sutton Middle School track team entered a packed stadium with hopes of leaving with a trophy that would symbolize their hunger to be the best at the sport but a fourteen year old undervalued adolescent felt differently and possessed a unique outlook on the day's events. This young lad was not sure if he possessed what was necessary to compete yet, ensued with a fire and desire that spoke of victory without its manifestation. He gathered his running shoes and proceeded to the starting gate when summoned by the announcer. Upon reaching the starting line and viewing the competition, he grew a bit discouraged because the runners all seemed bigger and stronger than he did. The announcer is heard over the PA system saying, "Ready, Set, as his arm raises complete silence fills the stadium and then POW the gun goes off and the runners sprint toward the finish line.

The young runner gives everything he has to the race and when the competitors all cross the finish line, he is the sole winner who led the pack and won the race. Can you imagine the feeling this young man must have felt doubting his ability to compete yet dousing the competition with his speed and strength? The thrill of victory is what the young runner experienced that day on the track and it forever changed how he approached upcoming races. When we experience the joys of healthy relationships, we are able to raise our hands in victory as we crossover the threshold from mediocre non-fulfilling relationships to exhilarating ones.

Building Blocks Creates Stepping Stones

I often say we must create building blocks that develop stepping-stones to escort us to the places in life that we wish to venture. When you are facing a difficult situation that is beyond your control, ask yourself, what steps are needed to begin the chain of events leading to eventual victory.

Fear can often times prohibit us from gaining the victory needed because we do not allow what we have inwardly to profess outwardly. If we are grounded in God, victory will come when you hold that ground.

When we are building, the process can be exhausting because the progress we desire materializes slowly but the old saying is "Good things comes to those who wait" I am a believer that amazing things are the reward of those who endure. Your building blocks of love, relationship and life will escort you to the stepping-stones of happiness and peace allowing you to live full and die empty.

When the foreman leads the charge of carpenters, contractors, builders and architects to construct a building the process can be tedious, but the entire team understands what the overall goals and objectives are and work tirelessly to build a solid structure. The attitude you take into building will determine what you will receive when construction is complete.

#KeepBuilding!!!

25 HIDING THE HURT WILL HINDER THE HEALING

If we Hide our Hurt we will Hinder God's Healing….A door closed doesn't allow light to enter the room…but a window ajar receives the wind of peace and the air of revitalization.

Parents are deemed gurus when it comes to hiding Christmas gifts, they do a fantastic job at keeping those gifts under lock and key until Christmas day and build excitement in their kids that resembles a mystery adventure in a fiction novel.

My mother must have purchased the "Hiding Christmas Gifts For Dummies" handbook because it seemed that every place my brothers and I would search we would come up empty. We lived in an apartment that had very little space to hide items so this magic trick left us perplexed.

My mother was like many of us who have been hurt; we have become magicians at hiding the truth and therefore have limited any notion of receiving healing. As tragic as heartbreak and disappointment can be, it is what happens afterwards that is more disturbing.

Have you ever been cut with a kitchen knife while chopping vegetables for dinner or by a sharp edge of paper? Those injuries be them small or great are painful for a number of reasons, they inflict agony that seems to last longer than the Titanic movie starring Leonardo DeCaprio and Kate Winslet, are nuisances, sting like crazy and seem to occur in places that will be bumped or touched throughout the day.

Many of us who have experienced any type of hurt either from a romantic relationship, a friendship, with a family member, at work or in the church, have dealt with it in its entirety or hidden fragments of it so resonant that deep-sea divers could not locate it. The issue with burying hurt is with it hidden, we are never given the opportunity to deal with its cause nor discover methods to move forward productively and receive the necessary closure to relinquish its residue. When something is hidden, it allows us to forget over time that it exists yet it remains present. A hidden treasure holds the same value as one discovered yet, it is the one discovered that receives the reward.

Hide and Go Seek

In my neighborhood we played a popular game called "Hide and Go Seek" it was a game where one person was chosen to be the seeker while all others were hiders. The seeker would count to a number giving the hiders a time limit to conceal their locations and challenge the seeker to find those hidden places and when found race back to the base to tag the hiders out of the game. This game was exhilarating and intriguing because hiders would create crafty niches to camouflage themselves and their location and it was always a race to the finish to see who would win the game or who would tag out first.

When we enter into relationships with hidden hurt, we have not only surrendered the opportunity for healing to commence but we have also transformed our partner involuntarily into the seeker racing throughout the relationship to find our authentic heart.

I experienced a great deal of hurt in a relationship that prompted me to forgo the phases of grief that researchers suggest we all experience. I took the news of our unexpected breakup in stride, acted as if it didn't faze me and once healed reflected on that relationship and wondered why.

I suppressed my feelings but they still existed. I was hurt beyond repair because I invested a great deal into the relationship and truly loved her with everything in me. I gave this woman more of me than I had with anyone else and I knew she was special because I often denied my own desires to fulfill hers. The devastation from that phone call (Oh Yes! she broke up with me over the phone) leveled me and somehow sent my hurt into the basement vault and I buried the key to the door. So why did I respond this way?

Digging through the Crates Finding a Classic

Back in the day when music was supreme and a house party was safe, the partygoers used a system of indulgence to determine if a Disc Jockey (DJ) at a party was good or great. His/her, ability to dig through the record crates for music that kept the crowd entertained throughout the event was always a deciding factor. This method allowed the DJ to funnel through music that held no substance to a crazed band of hyperactive young adults with no worries and plenty of food.

In order to receive healing from a hurtful incident we must dig deep into our emotional crates and play the music that will empower us to keep dancing throughout life. I am not suggesting that you ignore the process but that you seek the necessary restitution needed to proactively deal with your hurt and the hurtful situation.

Let the Healing Begin

After we go through the emotional roller coaster of feeling monotonous emptiness, recalling memories and anger due to the paper cuts of heartbreak we must do the following:

Stop the Bleeding- If we focus on the heartache for a long period of time the outpour of pain will continue and constantly remind of us the injury but also cause leakage into other aspects of our lives. We must create and install a drain stopper that we can utilize to seal the wounded areas of our hearts. This could include recreational activities, hobbies, meditation, etc.

Cleanse the affected area-Our hearts are delicate but powerful tools and store a great deal. If we do not properly clean the area most effected it may cause an infection that could prove more detrimental to our health than the original injury.

Allow the wound to air dry- We must allot the proper amount of time for our wounds to heal or we may find ourselves with an assortment of paper cuts that may shelve us from healthy relationships.

Get Antibiotics- If heartbreak isn't treated with a substance strong enough to kill the growth of bacteria better known as a "Cold Heart" the conditions of the wound could prove fatal to our social and professional lives.

Adam hid from God after he sinned because he says he was afraid and therefore, denied God the opportunity to reconcile him back to his rightful place preventing Adam from receiving restitution. Do not allow your fear of being hurt again cause you to hide your hurt precluding any prospect of healing to commence.

RESIDUE IN THE RELATIONSHIP 26

No, new wine must be poured into new wineskins. And no one after drinking old wine wants the new, for he says, 'The old is better.
Luke 5: 38-39

One evening on her way home from buying groceries my mother stopped at a fast food restaurant to pick up dinner, after ordering she realized that she did not have a safe place to store the dinner so she put the dinners in the bag along with the groceries once we arrived home and begin to unload the groceries we were shocked to learn that most of our dinner had spilled over into the bag with the groceries. This ordeal left a hefty mess and the residue from the mixture spoiled our dinner. Many of us are allowing residue from a previous relationship to spill over into our new and budding relationship and maybe tainting the new with the old.

Matthew 9:16-17 says, "No one sews a patch of unshrunk cloth on an old garment, for the patch will pull away from the garment, making the tear worse Neither do men pour new wine into old wineskins. If they do, the skins will burst, the wine will run out and the wineskins will be ruined. No, they pour new wine into new wineskins, and both are preserved." It seems like there is something about an old flame that carries into the new fire. I believe many of us experience this because we fail to totally cleanse ourselves of the previous relationship. It is almost equivalent to taking a bath but not emptying the tub completely only to have someone pour fresh water into the tub along with the existing used water that more than likely contains particles from your wash.

I recall as a kid going to the neighborhood candy store and buying the big dill pickle in a bag engulfed in a ton of pickle juice. It was a fun filled experience until the bag began to leak and as a kid I was not concerned about the bag or the leak, I found a new bag and put the existing bag in it. When we have leaks within our relationship or ourselves, we often step into a new situation without fixing the leak and therefore allow residue to seep into the relationship.

A Band-Aid Over A Hatchet Wound

Allowing issues to go unresolved is comparable to attempting to cover a hatchet wound with a band-aid. The damage caused by unresolved issues could prove detrimental to progress and continue the overage of dilution in your life. A hatchet wound requires surgery and stitches to repair the injury. Without the proper remedy for your wound(s), you allow seepage to drip into your fresh watered life damaging and tainting expecting growth.

The Coroner's Report

When my grandmother passed away in 2003, the coroner did the report issued on her death. A coroner is a government official who investigates human deaths, determines cause of death, issues death certificates, maintains death records and identifies unknown dead. Duties always include determining the cause, time, and manner of death. This uses the same investigatory skills of a police detective in most cases, because the answers are available from the circumstances, scene, and recent medical records. In many American jurisdictions, any death not certified by the person's own physician must be referred to the medical examiner. If an individual dies outside of his/her state of residence, the coroner of the state in which the death took place issues the death certificate.

After a relationship hazard, breakup or divorce we should utilize our internal investigative skills to conduct an autopsy to determine the cause of death, time and manner of which our relationship died. This will assist us in becoming a better mate and identifying areas of improvement. Many go through life like a gymnast on the exercise rings swinging from relationship to relationship without proper diagnosing the failures of the previous relationship therefore, possibly being the common denominator of the issues experienced in all of your futile relationships.

We must possess a tenacity to improve in all areas of our lives and more importantly procuring the proper amount of time in between dating or courting that will allow us to heal properly, assess appropriately and reemerge successfully.

CONFLICTS OF INTEREST 27

Building a quality relationship will take a hefty investment on your behalf, true commitment, time & effort.

A conflict of interest (COI) occurs when an individual or organization is involved in multiple interests, one of which could possibly corrupt the motivation for an act in the other. The presence of a conflict of interest is independent from the execution of impropriety. Therefore, a conflict of interest can be discovered and voluntarily defused before any corruption occurs.

Many of us struggle with love, commitment and building healthy relationships because we either have an internal or physical struggle with selfish desires. This occurs when we wrestles with our self worth and constantly wondering if we are good enough, rich enough or smart enough. A number of these issues are developed over time and can be caused by previous relationship or life experiences.

Men have a conflict of interest when it comes to the woman that they desire. He is interested but his interest conflicts with his intentions and his intentions conflicts with his motives, and his motives conflicts with his morals and so forth. This repetitive cycle does not allow him to commit completely to one woman therefore disabling him from being present in the relationship. Women have the same issue at times, the conflict is between the present and the past and this formula cooks up a nasty recipe for their future. They cannot commit themselves to the man that may compliment them because the conflict is challenging them to a battle within.

When a conflict of interest is present, it prevents men and women from productively progressing in any type of relationship and clouds the judgment of the two to make decisions that are for the betterment of the relationship.

When I first entered the music business, I was a young ambitious kid who wanted to be successful. My mother saw my drive and wanted to assist. She met an entertainment attorney who would share an interest in learning more about who I was and what my musical goals were. We spoke on the phone and later she invited my manager and I to her home for a more formal meeting. She was impressed with my abilities and scheduled a meeting with a label executive at his home. After a few half-hearted attempts and nervous rhetoric, I finally nailed the audition. The label signed me to a deal on the spot and we began recording. You may be asking what that has to do with conflicts of interests; well I am glad you asked! My mother developed a great relationship with the attorney and felt comfortable with her representing my interest as it related to legal business with my manager, contract with the label, etc. The problem was she also represented the label therefore; her interest and my mine would differ when it related to issues with the label.

Although the attorney did not appear to be manipulative her obligation was first to the label because she had a vested interest and they paid her hefty salary. I would soon learn where her loyalty lied when a dispute arose about my upcoming record and I wanted out of my contract.

The attorney quickly showed me which side her bread was buttered as she sided with the label and I found myself without a deal. If anything sounds out of place with this story, allow me to enlighten you. When I begin having issues with the record executives, I informed the attorney and she advised me to leave the label because she had several other labels that had shown interest. She said that if the label did not want to accommodate my menial requests then I should consider other options. The attorney spoke of major labels showing an interest in my project so I figured she was looking out for my future and I requested to be released from my contractual obligations. The record executive was not pleased but eventually obliged but during the heated struggle, the attorney turned on me, secured the interest of the label in our exit negotiations, and left me high and dry. I no longer had a recording contract or, any of the other labels she mentioned in previous conversations.

We must make sure that our mate or potential mate has our best interest in view long before we expose our vulnerabilities, strategies or emotional affection.

When conflicts of interest arise in your relationship, you must have complete certainty that your mate is for you and not against you. We must also assure that we have no other interests that will cause conflict once we commit to a relationship.

PART FIVE: HER LOVE

⏻ Power Point to Ponder

We cannot operate effectively in relationships half empty and must adequately assess what is missing from the relationship and us. Remember you cannot give what you do not own. If your heart is traumatically stoned from previous abuse, it may difficult to distribute the necessary love needed to develop anything short or long term. Allowing residue from previous encounters to rest in present endeavors will cause toxic results.

❓ Questions to Consider

Are you able to give or receive the love you desire? Are you experiencing similar results in every relationship? What fragile elements are causing repetitive behaviors in your relationships?

💎 Jewel Tip

Part-time lovers should not be rewarded with full-time benefits.

POWER NOTES:

PART SIX

HER MISSION

28 WHERE DOES THIS ROAD LEAD

Traveling with no destination will often land you in places of compromise producing loneliness, regret and destruction.

While living in Charlotte, NC I often found myself on streets that changed names quickly or lead to unknown places and I would ask "Where Does This Road Lead?" Many of us have asked or maybe currently asking that same question as it relates to the personal or professional road we are on at the moment. A GPS (Global Positioning System) is only as good as its master who gives it instructions to the destinations in which it calculates and issues directions. When we engage in relationships, business ventures or professional endeavors we are often questioning where it is leading us or have a perspective of where we want those ventures to lead us.

A friend of mine (whom we will call Dustin to protect the innocent) once shared with me his infidelity expedition, the roller coaster of emotions it placed him on and his road to recovery. In the end, he kept asking himself "Why" and I responded with a series of questions and answers that allowed him to see where the issue began and how he could sustain his redemptive stance and rebuild his marriage.

Dustin found himself entangled in a web of deception and on a one way street that eventually led to destruction and almost ruined everything he worked hard to build. Infidelity is a silent killer that destroys many lives yearly. Most people never see it approaching therefore, cannot properly prepare for the damage it will cause. Dustin shared that his secret love mania began as he entertained flirty advances from a coworker that eventually led to a full fledge affair. Dustin like many men who find themselves in a sordid relationship with a woman who is not their wife often wonder at times where the road is leading them and although they do not see a prosperous path, somehow cannot make the necessary detour and exit the freeway of lustful passion.

Can You Run The Distance

In high school I was on the track team and although I possessed a desire to run distance races I understood my ability and my lungs would not allow me to do so, therefore I became a sprinter because my talent allowed me to run in bursts of speed that exhausted after a certain distance. I admired many of my teammates including my good friend Derek "Fonzworth Bentley" Watkins, who had an amazing ability to run the distance with ease. He looked like a greyhound stretching the length of the track with every stride and seemed at times to operate from a ventilator of oxygen because he rarely seemed out of breath as he completed his races. The question our coach often asked was "Can You Run The Distance?" and for many like myself the answer was always NO!

When we venture into what I consider out of bound relationships we not only must view where the relationship may lead us but, are we prepared to run the distance. Life is full of a variety of adventures but none sets a roller coaster of emotions into play without properly preparing the players of its consequences and repercussions than an illicit affair. Women are wired differently from men and this is not a new discovery, yet it is a proven fact because of how God created us. We have varying functions but are equally valuable. We both have a need for love and that need often drives us to absorb unnecessary hits like a professional football player diving for a touchdown only to injure himself while falling short of the goal line.

The hopeful result of most courtships is marriage. When we are involved in relationships that have no proposed objectives, how do we envision the relationship unfolding? If a man is seeking a long-term relationship but the woman is enjoying the adventure or vice versa, one is not prepared to run the distance. The distance can be defined as the ultimate outcome. In some instances, that outcome is not favorable to the initiator and therefore causes him or her to falter. In the end, a wife or husband, child and, family are left with the devastation of a relationship that was built on lustful passion versus one that was carefully thought out.

Bret Farving

Brett Lorenzo Favre born October 10, 1969 is a former American football quarterback who spent the majority of his career with the Green Bay Packers of the National Football League (NFL). He was a 20-year veteran of the NFL, having played quarterback for the Atlanta Falcons (1991), Green Bay Packers (1992–2007), New York Jets (2008) and Minnesota Vikings (2009–2010). Favre is the only quarterback in NFL history to throw for over 70,000 yards, over 500 touchdowns, over 300 interceptions, and over 10,000 pass attempts. He officially retired on January 17, 2011.

In early March 2008, Favre announces that he is retiring from the Green Bay Packers. At a news conference, he said, "I know I can play, but I don't think I want to. It has been a great career for me, but it is over. As they say, all good things must end. I look forward to whatever the future may hold for me." Later in the month, Favre has second thoughts and wants to return.

This Bret Favre fiasco went on for two more years after his initial retirement and many around the league speculated that Favre merely wanted to see if he still had what it took to play in the NFL and possibly win another super bowl. How many men have scurried into the locker-room of retirement only to trot back on to the field to see if they are still considered desirable by women?

Married men often face this on again off again scenario where they are battling within themselves if they still possess the ability to attract women, turn them on romantically and entice them as they did in their heyday. The dangers of this thought process is it keeps men on the field attempting to play a game that has light years passed them by and with their diminished skills demonstrates that their egos have taken more abuse than football players who play long past their prime. It is nothing more disheartening than seeing an aged out boxer in the ring fighting for the glory days with burdens of making a payday only to suffer continuous embarrassment.

Once you have made a commitment to date exclusively or marry, you have relinquished your right to explore the possibilities, test the market of free agency or contend for the single life crown. You made a choice, so exploring what may be left in the tank to play the game is nonessential. The rationale factor is a selfish act and illustrates your level of maturity and value of your current relationship. Understand the more you invest in your current situation determines what return you will yield. Focus your attention on developing and growing where you are versus abandoning the blueprint or jeopardizing your entire portfolio altogether.

In The End Everyone Hurts

When we choose to participate in extracurricular activities (i.e. extramarital affairs) because of the pleasures within, we rarely foresee the damage those choices can cause. Adultery hurts everyone involved and although it may appear that all will be well when the spring fling, winter boo romance, summer sizzle or autumn escapade ends, the lasting affects echo beyond the sounds of passion and ultimately erodes the fibers of your relationship.

I once heard a story of a woman married to a pastor for twenty years only to find out that he was living a secret life with a woman in the church. The initial findings were damaging to the woman but the effects of the affair lasted over twenty years. The woman never truly healed from the trauma caused by her husband the pastor and has found it difficult to trust or love again.

What a miserable way to live. This happens to men and women across the globe daily and those responsible never consider the ongoing distress their selfish choices may cause. I have been on the giving and receiving end of an affair and today years after the dust has settled from the act my selfish decisions reverberates consequences. I think about the beginning of my journey and how it ended but it's the in between that positions me to share with you that today's choices may be tomorrow's regrets and we must consider everyone's feelings and make better choices.

In life there are no do over's, we can only rewind video appliances such as television DVR's, DVD players, streaming video on YouTube or Daily Motion but cannot rewind life's choices. We must learn from life's choices and cease to duplicate them. Remember your mate has feelings just as you do and Pepto-Bismol only cures heartburn not heartaches or heartbreaks.

NOT SICK BUT SINGLE

29

Our skills and talents make us tools but our failures and shortcomings remind us that we need a craftsman in control of our lives.

Have you ever witnessed people at the doctor's office who did not present any physical or mental signs of having an ailment? Men and women often view being single as a sickness; they rummage around seeking a date doctor to assist them in finding true love. This mythical method of finding solace in a mate could be the reasons why so many are not married who desire to be.

Being single can be a depressing state or an exhilarating one, depending on how you view it. Rather than moping around because you have no one to love, recognize your freedom to see the world and live your dreams. You have an opportunity for a voyage of self-discovery that may elude those who are in relationships. Make the most of your single status by developing the confidence that comes from loving yourself and your life.

Living Single was an American television sitcom, which aired for five seasons on the Fox network from August 29, 1993 to January 1,

1998. The show centers on the lives of six friends who share personal and professional experiences while living in a Brooklyn brownstone. The show displayed the ups and downs of six friends experiencing life on the single road while enjoying the lessons life taught them through those experiences. This show allowed men and women across the globe to experience joyful and exhilarating moments *"Living Single"*. It demonstrated to viewers the varying options they had to live a fruitful single life.

It seems the later in life people are single the more they began to worry if they will ever find a mate and marry.

For many people, being single has been an on-off phase in their lives. Even after marriage, many people still split up because of the myriad of reasons that cause a break up. These ugly break-ups leave both parties alone most of the time and in many cases, unhappy. What many fail to understand is being single does not mean you have to be unhappy. You can find happiness even without a partner.

Being single is not the end of the world. You have lived through many phases in your life when you were single and survived. There are many things that single people can do or be part of to enjoy his or her life.

In order for you to be content with being single, you will need to remember the following:

Stay out of the rearview mirror: Past is past. You should focus more on what lies ahead for you in life versus what you left behind. You can never replace what has already occurred, but you can always create something new.

Be Grateful for the storms and celebrate the sunshine: Several aspects of your life give light and happiness to you although; it can be difficult to manage the heartache of a breakup. Acknowledge the treasures you have at your disposal (i.e. friends, family, co-workers, etc.) and utilize those as a valuable source of love, attention and support that you may need during your single life.

Your hourglass is ticking slowly: More time, less pressure. You are able to enjoy more free time, explore adventures and experience new and exciting things. Allowing the pressure from friends or family to get married will cause you to make permanent decisions based upon temporary situations. You are in control, allow life to move with you versus you moving at the rate that your life scenarios may be offering.

Who's loving you: The Jackson 5 had a hit song entitled "Who's Loving You" in which the charismatic lead singer consistently wondered who was loving the woman that he mistreated. You must learn to love yourself. During your time apart and without a mate take, time to learn more about yourself, do things you love to do and enjoy the freedom of being YOU!

Get out your scale: You must weigh the pros and cons of your situation. You may be single by choice or by circumstance, either way there is an upside to your single living. Think about the strains a relationship entails, and how much freedom you are experiencing as a single man/woman. Look at the good points and weigh the bad ones and you should be able to conjure up an effective remedy to assist you with your status.

30 MARRIAGE MATERIAL

The material used to build a marriage will ultimately determine its durability. Those built on shallow surfaces may be susceptible to rapid decline at an alarming rate. Those built on a sturdy cliff may tilt but will not tip over completely.

Are you Marriage Material? Asking this question to any man or woman would most likely generate a response that is edifying to the one responding. Many may assume that they are the proper material for marriage but are they really.

When God decided to flood the earth because of its sinful nature, he chose Noah, a righteous man, blameless among the people of his time to replenish it. God instructed Noah to build a boat and included what types of material he wanted utilized to construct it. He told Noah to make the boat of gopher wood and seal it inside and out with tar. While there is no definition for what exactly gopher wood is, we can assume that it was a strong and sturdy type of wood that could withstand the rigorous task of securing Noah, his family and all the animals chosen by God to replenish the earth.

My good friend actor and bestselling author, Hill Harper often shared a story of two houses while addressing his audience as we toured the country with UNCF on its Empower Me Tour. He would say there are two houses that were built on different coasts with different material, one made of wood while the other was constructed using brick. The two houses were developed for the conditions in which they were being built to withstand. One would endure grueling temperatures while the other needed to resist the moving of the earth during earthquakes. He would often see if the audience could guess which house was built for which condition.

When we seek to marry, we must be able to withstand the trials, attacks, along with the daily temptations that may arise in our marriages and must encompass the fortitude to persist.

What type of material you become will be determined by what ingredients are utilized. If superficial ingredients are used, your building materials will not be able to withstand the atmosphere. If you allow God to pour into your foundation and seal you inside and out with his anointed tar, you will be able to weather any storm sent in your direction.

God gave marriage as a gift to Adam and Eve. They were created perfect for each other. Marriage was not just for convenience, nor was it brought about by any culture. It was instituted by God and has three basic aspects:

(1) The man leaves his parents and, in a public act, promises himself to his wife.
(2) The man and woman are joined together by taking responsibility for each other's welfare and by loving the mate above all others.
(3) The two are united into one in the intimacy and commitment of sexual union that is reserved for marriage.

The bible suggests that in order to have a strong marriage you would need to include all three.

What makes people marriage material? One may insinuate that having a strong financial portfolio and stability would classify you for candidacy however, I find the bible's definition to be more appealing. Although man was created first scriptures say in Genesis 2:18 *"Then the LORD God said, "It is not good for the man to be alone. I will make a helper who is just right for him."*

God's creative work was not complete until he made woman. He could have made her from the dust of the ground as he made man. God chose however, to make her from the man's flesh and bone. In doing so, he illustrated for us that in marriage man and woman symbolically are united into one. This is a mystical union of the couple's heart.

I believe the following qualifies people for marriage:
- Possessing the ability to endure the hurricane seasons of marriage
- Understanding its purpose
- Recognizing personal faults, strengths and weaknesses
- Having a desire to satisfy and serve your mate without expectations
- Developing the proper attitude and motives for marriage

Instituting Self-Love

When we think about self-love many may avert to a love that is self-serving or selfish. Unlike the aforementioned self-love is described in Romans 13:9 saying, *"For this, Thou shalt not commit adultery, Thou shalt not kill, Thou shalt not steal, Thou shalt not bear false witness, Thou shalt not covet; and if there be any other commandment, it is briefly comprehended in this saying, namely, Thou shalt love thy neighbor as thyself.(KJV)"*.

Somehow many of us have gotten the notion that self-love is wrong. If this were true in the sense that God defines the above scripture would be pointless. How could you love your neighbor as you love yourself if you did not possess self-love? The bible says even when you have low self-esteem; you probably do not willingly let yourself go hungry. You take care of your body and may even exercise. You clothe yourself, make sure you have a roof over your head and protect yourself against injuries at all costs. This type of love we must possess for others and our mate. Loving others as we love ourselves mean actively working to see that we meet their needs. We must institute the self-love mechanism, which will allow us to treat our mate as we treat ourselves.

Revive the Art of Courtship

I have often heard many stories of men and women meeting only to act like husband and wife months later, or a woman desiring a man and he wants to jump into bed before really getting to know her. I believe men and women are so thirsty for companionship and intimacy that they fail to date each other like generations before. Dating a woman is the same as the old school term of "courting her". The new generations of social media driven relationships are built on a number of things and many of those things lack courtship. Courtship is not some secret method of wooing a woman but it is seeking the affections of a woman usually with the hope of marriage and if you are interested in her heart, it will be more beneficial to you and your relationship to do so. You can court a woman with civility, respect and a few unpretentious guidelines. There are four ingredients to courtship:
1. Action
2. Time Frame
3. Pursuance
4. Response of a Woman

First, you must take action; go after the woman you desire so that you will not have to settle for the available woman. Secondly, be patient because courting will take time to develop a solid foundation. So many are microwaving relationships versus slow roasting it in the oven and allowing the tender and delicate moments of the relationship to take shape. Thirdly, pursue her. Go after her with intent to make her an honorable woman meaning you see her as valuable and not just another notch on the old belt. Finally, allow her to respond to you and the developing stages of the relationship. Not all women are the same, therefore, will not give you the exact experiences of others. You must exercise patience in allowing her to connect with you overall.

As you court her, remember to stay present in the relationship. Explore getting to know her without sex. Society teaches that a relationship is not truly healthy without a good antidote of sex, but I strongly disagree. If you are truly after her heart, the chambers of her cookie jar are not as important. There are Do's and Don'ts in courting a woman not that there is one particular formula that works however, the following should help point you in the right direction.

- **Do special things for her:** Doing things *"Just Because"* will demonstrate your intentions for her long-term. If your aim is a quick fix of pleasure, I suggest you stop reading right now because none of what I am sharing will assist you with that. If you want to capture her attention, do special things that are innovative, exclusive (not this worked with *Summer* so I will do the same with *June*), and heartfelt.
- **Be interested in more than her cup size:** engage an attentive ear, discuss and, learn more about who she is as a person, her background, what is important to her, her fears, her doubts about life, relationships and business,

etc. When you consistently show an interest in her as a woman, you will fall in love with every aspect, not just her physical attributes.

- **Create a think tank:** Create an atmosphere that consistently allows her to grow and learn while she learns and grows. This creative mechanism allows her to learn more about you and herself while displaying in her mind how the two of you may connect long-term and sealing in her heart your true motives for pursuing her.

For Better or Worse

I often wonder do those who aspire to marry truly understand what the duties of moving from the single season of life into becoming a husband or wife mean. I often joke with friends that marriage will present the worse long before we see the better, but this statement is very true.

Adam was alone with all of the animals God created when God realized that it was not good for Adam to be by himself and therefore created woman. The interesting part of this creation is that he formed her from the rib of man versus the soil of the ground as he did all other creations. *You may ask what that scenario has to do with the subtitle. Continue reading and you will soon discover my poignant point.* The bible says that man and woman were created perfect for each other, so how is it that so many men and women are not able to endure the challenges of marriage and end up divorced.

I believe people are in love with the idea of marriage and often exhaust so much of themselves, their finances and their emotions into the wedding that they have little to give to the longevity of the marriage itself. I've heard people say things like "We fell out of love with one another", "I'm no longer happy in this relationship" or "I love him/her but I'm not in love with them". It is not that we have fell out of love, I am not even sure that is possible but I believe we have failed to educate ourselves on the grand purpose of marriage and what we are called by God to accomplish as a couple. Furthermore, during the marriage, we discontinue all or most of the methods and mechanics we utilized during the dating period to entice, enlighten and, enhance the relationship.

Marriage is a continual work in progress and a classroom for learning intricate details about your mate that allows you to continue growing together. In order to become prime marriage material you must understand what it will take to fulfill the "Until death do we part" portion of the marital vows that God expects us to honor.

The worse in a marriage is what seemingly seasons the better to taste like your favorite dinner dish. It is through those moments that we honestly illustrate who we are as husbands and wives and ultimately, sets the tone for the duration of the marriage.

God designed for marriage to work the problem is many who marry are not prepared to work the marriage. At the first sign of trouble, we often utilize the exit clause that God allowed Moses to issue failing to understand his purpose in restoring the marriage and reconciling us back to him.

God longs to restore man, hence his declaration of grace and mercy and his redemptive nature and requirement of us to repent. If he meant for it to go any other way he would not have sent his only begotten son to die for our sins. It is always God's goal for us to reconcile and restore our marriages as he does with us daily. We must adapt the fortitude and implement the patience to work as much on our marriages as we do our careers.

Do not allow your selfish motives to propel you to the divorce court. God expects you to seek him and his righteousness as it relates to you and your relationship so that his work may be made perfect in you. Others will join his kingdom because you have demonstrated through your marriage what God is able to do if we lean not unto our own understanding and acknowledge him in all our ways.

Three's Company...Three's A Crowd

Three's Company is an American sitcom that aired from 1977 to 1984 on ABC. The story revolved around three single roommates who all platonically shared an apartment in Santa Monica, California. The show chronicled the escapades of the trio's constant misunderstandings, social lives, and struggle to keep up with rent. When Three's Company eventually ended it birthed, a spin off entitled Three's A Crowd. I loved the slapstick comedy of John Ritter and in both shows, he often displayed a humor that drew viewers in to his character and made him seem like a well-known relative. Although Ritter's character Jack enjoyed the tantalizing life of a bachelor entertaining two women in the sitcom, introducing such antics into your relationship could prove catastrophic. Many believe it is every man's dream to bring another woman into his bedroom with his wife but that is not true. Many men are content with satisfying their mate only. He may have entertained the thoughts of having a ménage á trois at points in his life but has found solace with his mate and would never invite it into his relationship.

While many men and women believe they should go to great lengths to please their mate, we must be careful of what we introduce into our marriage. Hebrews 13:4 says, *"Marriage is honorable in all, and the bed undefiled: but whoremongers and adulterers God will judge."* Many men and women have invited a third party into their bedroom only to have their mate continue with outside activities afterward. The flesh is never satisfied and the more we feed it, the hungrier it will get. We must become all that our spouse needs so that his or her desires stay within the parameters that God intended.

Giving Up the I for We

Deuteronomy 24:5 says *"When a man hath taken a new wife, he shall not go out to war, neither shall he be charged with any business: but he shall be free at home one year, and shall cheer up his wife which he hath taken"*. Many enter into marriage with an independent mindset and wonder why things go south quickly. Marriage was not designed for individuals to operate independent of their spouses. In the biblical days, the man was expected to be home with his bride for at least one year without any outside distractions. Today, so many businessmen and women, entertainers and, everyday couples are placing their needs above the needs of their marriage. Women are executives these days and spend hours at the office working during the first year of their marriage while their husband is left to care for himself. Not that it is wrong for a woman to have a career of her own but, if we desire fruitful marriages, we must invest as God has instructed us in order to receive the benefits he has promised our marriages. Men are away from the home conducting a variety of tasks within the first year of their marriages and leaving their wives uncovered and protected from the temptations of the enemy whose primary goal is to kill, steal and destroy.

God required newly married couples to remain together with no distractions the first year of their marriage to avoid placing an excessive burden upon a new, unproven relationship and, to give it an opportunity to mature and strengthen before confronting it with numerous responsibilities. A gardener starts a tiny seeding in a small pot and allows it to take root before planting it in the field. You must allow your marriage to grow strong by protecting your relationship from too many outside distractions and pressures especially in the beginning.

Marriages were built to last forever according to the gospel. Although, God allowed Moses to issue a decree of divorce he is not in favor of couples divorcing. Many often say "I Chose The Wrong Mate" I disagree. I believe the mate you choose to marry God will honor his word concerning marriage. You must understand the process in which you will endure to complete your marriage according to God's word. It is not that you have chosen the wrong mate; it is that you have chosen not to allow God's word to work within you. We often grow impatient when the honeymoon period of our relationship has ended. We begin to see cracks in the armor of the mate we deemed a superhero and our fantasy of what we envisioned the marriage being has turned into a sordid mystery resembling a bad movie with less talented actors. The issue is not the marriage yet, it is the people in the marriage.

We cannot do what we want and expect God to fix all of our bad choices. Remember, you chose your mate and therefore should take the process of selecting your mate more seriously. The things you see early on that you know you cannot live with will not change because you say "I Do". If you choose to walk down the aisle and commit to everlasting life with your spouse, you must also be prepared to commit to the work that is required to make everlasting life a reality.

We must do the following while we are waiting for a mate or in search of one:

- Learn God's definition of marriage
- Understand his principles and purpose
- Work on becoming a selfless mate versus a selfish one
- Prioritize your life to include a mate long before you consider marriage
- Become skilled at communicating well
- Learn conflict resolution
- Store God's word in your heart so that you may not sin against him (psalm 119:11)

MARRYING JEZEBEL

31

But if you refuse to serve the LORD, then choose today whom you will serve. Would you prefer the gods your ancestors served beyond the Euphrates? Or will it be the gods of the Amorites in whose land you now live? But as for me and my family, we will serve the LORD."
Joshua 24:15

The delight of finding a queen that loves you wholeheartedly, cares for your well-being is priceless but the agonizing discovery of a woman who is evil, manipulative and controlling is not. Ahab was the eighth king of Israel, a capable leader and military strategist who lacked discipline and maturity and allowed his wife Jezebel to influence him to do evil.

Ahab was trapped by his own choices, and he was unwilling to take the right action. So was his wife to blame for his decisions? Although, Jezebel had a vice grip on Ahab's heart, he still possessed the power and authority to make better choices but chose not to in order to satisfy his greed and sinful desires.

Jezebel ranks as the most evil woman in the bible and people often equate her to that of a loose woman, flimsy and a bit raunchy with men but Jezebel was far from that. She was a determined woman who married into Israel, brought her pagan god with her and was unwavering in making all of Israel worship her gods. Jezebel's one outstanding "success" was in contributing to the eventual downfall of the northern kingdom-idolatry. God punished the northern tribes for their idolatry by having them carried off into captivity. She held great power. Jezebel not only managed her husband but she also had 850 assorted pagan priests under her control. Jezebel was committed to herself and her gods.

A woman who has other beliefs aside from her husband will cause dissent. Her gods governed Jezebel and caused her husband to stumble and fall as Eve did with Adam.

You must carefully choose the woman you will marry and look at the entire woman versus a few benefits you discover while dating. While a woman who is strong and committed are desirable traits, the bigger question would be, whom is she committed to and where is she utilizing her strengths?

If Jezebel possessed those phenomenal traits and served the one true God that, her husband originally served their house would have been able to do wondrous things.

Political Influence

Women are like politicians, they hold a great deal of influence and power and the ability to shift things quickly. Eve persuaded Adam to go against what he knew was right jezebel influenced her husband Ahab, and a nation of people to indulge in Baal worship and the married prostitute lured men into her bed while her husband was away on business leading them to a painful death. God said that it was not good for man to dwell alone therefore, he caused man to fall into a deep sleep and extracted woman from his rib creating an immediate bond that allows her to have access to his heart.

Women are created to protect a man's heart and his interests but also at times, women have used their gifts and power to wrongly influence men to do evil.

Politicians have developed a reputation for over promising and under delivering which taints their word as viewed by voters, and therefore, they have to work harder to prove their commitment to the community in which they vowed to serve. We must escape the label of building unhealthy relationships with ulterior motives that destroy the sanctity of marriage and the origin of God's original intent for marriages.

The Running Mate

In the 2008 Presidential race, GOP presidential candidate Senator John McCain presumed to change the game when he elected Governor Sarah Palin of Alaska as his running mate to battle presidential hopefuls Senator Barack Obama and Joe Bidden for the presidency. Many questioned the senator's choice at a rally but McCain told the crowd that Palin was "*exactly who I need*" and "*exactly who this country needs to help us fight the same old Washington politics of me first and country second*".

"*For the last few months I've been looking for a running mate who can best help me shake up Washington and make it start working again. It is with great pride that I tell you that I have found the right partner to help me stand up to those who value their privilege over their responsibility or power over principle, who put their interests over your needs.*"

The plan his team devised seemed to be in full swing and gaining momentum on the Obama campaign until they put Governor Palin in front of the media and realized that she was not as equipped as they hoped to handle the scrutiny of the media or the influx of information provided to tackle the campaign issues. There was also speculation based upon information released by former campaign staff, that Palin began to go against what the campaign stood for and that caused a rift between the golden two to become leaders of the free world.

The mistake that the McCain campaign made was not in choosing Governor Palin but allowing themselves to be placed in a situation that pressed them to gallop into the dark not knowing what they were really getting with Palin and, not adequately preparing her for the circus she would experience because of her decision to accept the nomination.

We must thoroughly investigate the mate we plan to spend the rest of our lives with in order to determine if they are truly a fit for our long-term campaign of marriage. If we fail to do so, we may experience a great deal of turbulence once the marriage campaign gets going and that may prove fatal when our lives are in front of others who can see the truth disclosed behind a façade of political jargon.

32 JUST BEING A MAN

Jesus answered, "It is written: 'Man does not live on bread alone, but on every word that comes from the mouth of God. Matthew 4:4

How many times have you heard a man say these diabolical words, "I'm just being a man" and that statement when attached to an action that somehow involves him making trivial decisions that affects others? As strange as this scenario may be to some, it is all too familiar to others and has plagued men for centuries. It is a detriment to those who are seeking a mate untainted by the immature behavior of men who are taught to make excuses for their behavior and consider that behavior a rite of passage, when in fact; it is counterproductive to building healthy relationships.

I often cringe at hearing men consistently make excuses for their actions because I know and understand that those actions have caused and or will cause destruction in the lives of the women who sincerely care about them.

I myself have fallen into the web of thinking more is better and learned the hard way that less is more. It is like being in the water on a raft at the beach and thinking to yourself that you only want to venture so far into the cold quenching stream only to close your eyes and find yourself a great deal further than expected. So why is it that men feel as though they cannot escape the onslaught of beautiful, sexy and, alluring women who may present themselves as gifts? Being a man involves a great deal more than merely having the ability to sleep with a number of women and the prognosis that we have been given that engaging in multiple sexual relationships actually prepares us for manhood is preposterous.

Truth is chasing things that only satisfy the flesh will only push you to desire more of the dangers you seek but will not ever quench the thirst.

A good deal of women expect men to cheat because that has been the extent of their experience with men and in such instances she has witnessed a cycle of repetition from either her father, step-father, brother or uncle. So is the case with men who venture into the adult world of exotic exploits. Many of them were taught that having multiple women distinguished them as men and that nothing is wrong with having such an experience. Unfortunately, many of us are taught the wrong lessons and women have suffered because of our ignorance. Therefore, what does being a man entail? A man is responsible, strong, loving. He is a provider of both emotional and financial support. He aims to cater to those he loves and he is adaptive. I may not have listed everything that I believe make up the qualities of a man but you get the picture.

I believe that men must erase the chalkboard of memory and habitual habits to improve the overall status of men in our society. The "Just Being A Man" campaign has garnered men a nasty reputation that many believe will never regain its original essence and although that may be true, I believe we can improve greatly and put a serious dent in the debt we owe to women.

You will need a few tools in your toolbox to accomplish this feat and I have included them below:

1. **Commit to Growth**- You must commit to growing as a man. Be consistent in adopting habits that will allow growth and develop in your character.
2. **Combat Negative Traits**- To grow properly and rapidly you must identify and rectify negative traits about yourself that may limit your forward progress
3. **Discover You**- Often we are molded into the men someone desired us to be without knowing who we are ideally. Once you have discovered your identity, begin to live it.
4. **Find A Mentor**- No man is an island. You must enlist someone whom you admire or has achieved what you desire and build a rapport.
5. **Enhance Your Skills**- Equip yourself with more skills. Skills enable you to be more productive and pull opportunities in your direction. Learn something new and strengthen your current skills. The more you learn the better you will become.
6. **Define Your Nucleus**- If you do not have a clear set of values defined, you can find yourself drifting along in life. This will prevent you from making consistent bad choices and will breed confidence.
7. **Prioritize**- You must order your life steps and govern your decisions based upon most important to least.

Understanding where you begin in life is not necessarily where you have to end allows you to make the proper modifications to your life to become a better man, friend, brother and husband. I have given you trinkets that will assist you in becoming a better man, now I will give you tools to assist you in becoming a better husband or boyfriend.

1. **Become skilled at hearing silence**- You must learn her quiet signals. Hear the many levels of her speech that are like a dog whistle for humans. By the time, she has to give you instructions you have already missed several hints.
2. **Don't Lose You in the Tunnel of Love-** Do not lose your sense of individuality. Becoming one spirit does not negate you from being an individual. Losing your individuality causes the relationship to lose something special...You!
3. **Never use force, foul language or your fist**- It is **NEVER** ok to use violence or foul language towards your wife. If the relationship gets to a point where yelling is your only option or answer then you have made a mistake somewhere along the lines and it is time to regroup.
4. **No Keith Sweat with sex** - Keith Sweat was an 80's Rhythm and Blues singer known for his petitioning women for sex (in other words he was a beggar for sex). You must create moments that present romantic elements that produce enjoyable sex for all parties. Duty booty will only satisfy you but she will soon loathe those intimate moments you desire.
5. **Be Pleasant**- No woman likes an arrogant man. Be warm, kind, positive, understanding, friendly and patient. You must be sensitive to your surroundings at all times and respond accordingly.
6. **Dependable, accountable and compassionate-** Every woman wants her man to be reliable, someone she can count on no matter what. Provide comfort when she may be feeling despondent. Do not demean or hurt her self-esteem. If she is employed, understand her work

pressures and problems. Be enriching to her accomplishments and admire her often.
7. **Reverence the Vows**- Faithfulness and devotion is what a wife needs from her husband. Have a sense of honor and duty. Remain committed and if you should fall short refer to chapter 35 for atonement.

Being a good husband or boyfriend is something that is continuously evolving. You must actively participate in your own rescue and not fall into the mundane operation of daily monotony.

THE SHORT GAME

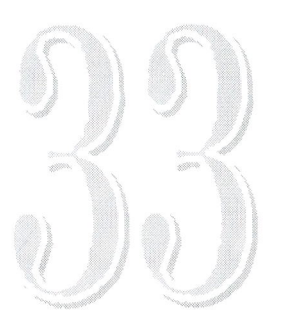

33

We prepare for life minus the curve ball changes it may throw...when change shows up just get in the car and ride shotgun!

I have loved to play the game of pool since I was a teenager but because my mother felt that pool was a dirty game she never allowed me to play, therefore I did not learn how to play well enough to win consistently. My infatuation with the game of pool was very intense, I would watch televised games where players were making shots from behind their backs, curving balls to jump over other balls, and creating unbelievable shots in order to win the game. Pool was infectious to me. I noticed in one particular match a player utilized his short game to win the match and it allowed me to see something for the first time in the game of pool that related to life and relationships. The player's short game strategy shifted his focus from frivolous play to the options that were in front of him. He picked his shots according to what he saw first and not what was best for him long-term throughout the game.

How many of us have chosen a mate based upon what we saw first and not on what was best for us long-term? The rhetorical question posed simply says that we have often chosen options that merely looked good at first sight but, without properly investigating, the return on the investment we would make and in some cases, it utterly cost us our life savings. Men and women are in search of companionship and that quest often disconnects our ability to think logically. When we meet people of interest, it forfeits any thoughts of longevity because our adept ability summons us to live in the moment. The problem with living in the moment at times is that the moment will surely pass by and we are left holding the bag of whatever it blew in when it landed in our lap and that at times is a bag of manure, stinking up our lives for many years to come.

Long-Term Investing vs. Short-Term Trading

Stockbrokers share in the rewards of its clients investing in short-term stocks versus long-term maturity stocks, which often may take a longer period to pay dividends than those short-term trading.

"Buy and hold" is a term that refers to long-term investing. A long-term hold, as defined by the Internal Revenue Service for tax purposes, owning a stock position for one year or longer. Theoretically, the longer you hold a stock, the more likely you will ride through periods of volatility and eventually enjoy profits as the underlying company grows. This based on the presumption that a good company will continue to grow its business and revenues over time and the stockholders will participate in that growth through stock price appreciation. Long-term holding also applies to dividend-paying stock that will continue to provide dividend income over the long-term.

Short-term trading is not limited to day trading. The IRS defines short-term holdings as those that sold within one year of their purchase. A short-term holding of a stock is primarily associated with trading the stock to take advantage of short-term market volatility that produces a quick profit.

The difference in long-term investing versus short-term trading is obvious. With one, you endure a period of maturity while the other offers a quicker return. In relationships, it may be foolish to enter with a short-term trading mentality expecting the results of a long-term investment. While it is safe to say that the taxes associated with the relationships we enter varies nevertheless, we are taxed and for some heavier than others. Tax treatment of short-term and long-term holding periods is different. Short-term capital gains taxed at a higher rate than long-term capital gains primarily because over a period your mate will see and understand your commitment to building a healthy portfolio versus simply looking to cash in on a curvaceous stock that seems full of delicacies and edible fruits.

My point in this comparison is that we often do not consider the benefits or downfalls of how we enter relationships before emotions are introduced. In the stock market, while short-term trading may seem enticing as it presents the possibility of quick profits, it takes considerable skill to time the market. It also costs a lot of money to pay the transaction fees for numerous trades within a short period of time, which shrinks your profits. It is costly to delve into a number of short-term relationships versus the profitability of a long-term investment.

Winning Is Everything

As a child playing sports, coaches often shared their philosophy on winning being the primary objective to playing the game. However, depending upon the game you play, it will determine if winning is everything. Many men feel as though getting as many women as possible is winning or plotting to get a woman in bed quickly is a huge win for his #Team_Sex_Em_Fast. I believe winning is when a man presents himself as a viable option for a woman and treats her as if she was an expensive jewel, caring for her delicately and insuring her safety in case of unforeseen heartbreak.

The popular movie "Grown Ups" starring Adam Sadler, Kevin James, Chris Rock, David Spade and Rob Schneider is a film about five childhood friends who won their junior high basketball championship. During the celebration at a rented lake house, their coach "Buzzer" (Blake Clark) encourages them to live their lives in a similar way to how they played the game. Thirty-two years later, the five friends, who had remained close companions up until graduation, have since separated. When their coach passes away, they all return to the lake house to celebrate his death and catch up with one another. In one scene, Sadler has a teaching moment with his son. The school bully and his family challenged the five friends to a basketball rematch of their junior high championship. The bully, arbitrarily landed on hard times when he lost his job and although they were obnoxious needed a break. Sadler ultimately figures out that his life has seen many more rewards than the bully and his family and at a pivotal point when he could win the game; he decided to miss the game winning shot and allow the bully and his family to win instead. When asked by his son why he deliberately missed the shot in a crucial moment he replied, "I wanted them to know what it felt like to win". If we treated our mates as Sadler did his rival, we would experience heaven in our relationships.

Winning is everything and sometimes winning is not crossing the finish line first, drilling a half-court basket at the buzzer, scoring the go-ahead touchdown or hitting a grand slam in the ninth inning. Winning is denying yourself the thrill of personal victory for the sake of allowing someone else the opportunity to feel triumphant.

34 QUALITY VERSUS QUANTITY

Having more of something is not equal to having the best of something.

Society has painted a distorted picture of the quality of life. Many feel that having a magnitude of things equates to having the best of things. I have always believed that I would rather have the quality of something versus a quantity of something. The markets are flooded with replica name brand purses, shoes, clothing and entertainment. I have a friend who enjoys watching movies and often purchases them while running errands or at the barbershop. He likes to purchase bootleg DVD's...I mean copyright infringed material for you scholars. The issue aside from the obvious legal ramifications is often the quality is horrible and does not allow true enjoyment of the films.

In life, you want to work on building quality relationships be it both personally and professionally versus a quantity of meaningless, shallow and unfulfilling ones. Good workers take pride in the quality and beauty of their work. God is concerned with the quality and beauty of what we do. Regardless of your status socially or professionally, you should strive to build quality versus quantity.

Take pride in building an exemplary relationship that many around you will not only envy but also desire. This will afford you an opportunity to teach others how to build quality based relationships that cater to the up building of both parties involved and focuses more on team building versus individuals sports. I love giving sport analogies because I feel many can relate regardless if they are sports fans or not.

In many instances, quantity would suffice such as money to start a business, buy a home, or in a corporation where you may have a quantity of workers but their quality of work suffers greatly. In your quest to build quality personal relationships, you will need to exercise the quality factor versus the quantity factor.

The following may assist you with determining what you will need:

1. **Supplementary dating opportunities**- You may go on a quantity of dates and those dates may produce a higher quantity of contacts that could give you more opportunities to find high quality prospects. But, if those dates lack the qualities that align with your goals, they could prove to be a waste of time and energy.
2. **Value of your network**- Assess what you have in your existing potential personal/professional network. Often times we may find someone we overlooked that has high quality and possess the ability to produce a quantity of things for us.
3. **Diversify your portfolio**- Occupying a diverse quantity of dating prospects will increase your chances of finding a quality mate with varying assets.

Lottery Ticket

The lottery commission experienced a whirlwind of participants when it hit a record payout of $656 million dollars in 2012. When the ticket fell, none of its three winners came forward immediately. Many wondered if the winners were aware that they had in their possession the winning ticket or afraid to come forth for fear of how many unknown relatives they would encounter. Many of you may be holding in your possession the winning ticket or you are the winning ticket waiting for your mate or potential mate to lay claim to you. Regardless of your position today, you are a lottery pick and similar to the draft in professional sports, many teams are clamoring to get to the top of the charts to select you. Consistently develop your quality so that your quantity of blossoming characteristics will speak volume.

WHY SINGLE WOMEN DATE MARRIED MEN

35

We must be careful of the choices we choose be they foolish or wise for the consequences may prove to be substantial.

One of the most unanswered questions to date and perhaps the most controversial is "Why Does Single Women Date Married Men"? In 2011, the wife of her alleged boyfriend Antwaun Cook accused American Idol winner Fantasia Barrino of being a home wrecker. As this news satirized blogs sites and newswires across the country, many of her fans were asking the question, "Why single women date married men?" Barrino not only supposedly dated the married man but also wound up pregnant and, subsequently taken to court by the estranged wife for breaking up their happy home. Paula Cook cited that Fantasia was the antiquated legal cause of Antwuan's alienation of affection towards her and she wanted custody of the couple's two children plus alimony and child support.

Researchers and bloggers have interviewed, polled and, pondered whether it is a fantasy, fetish or foolish preference. We have all heard various reasons. Some single women say they date married men because it is easy and that they are not looking for a commitment at the time. If this is solely the case and single women are not looking for a commitment then why chose someone who is supposed to be committed for life? Why doesn't she choose a single man? How easy can it be to be in a relationship with a married man? Are we to assume that her reasons are primarily that it gives her something to do from time to time? Feelings have to play a factor into the equations somehow, because after all does she really like him because he was easy? It is something about that married man that drew her to him in the first place. So what is it?

Several reasons come to mind when analyzing this situation, which are money, romance and sex. If she needs money from him, then she does not care if he is married or not because her goal is to obtain financial security and therefore, her morality disposition is secondary. His romantic prowess based upon what he says to her or how he responds to her essential needs could be a factor in her assessment to make him a fixture in her private life. Regardless if she meets him at the office, church or in a public place, several things about him could be grounds for her to engage in a relationship.

In my quest to bring about the truth without any condemnation I spoke with several women who shared their reasons for jumping on the infidelity bandwagon and I have withheld identifies to protect the forgiven from the persecution many would render.

Meet Sheila, who discussed with me her experience with Daryl the office executive. Sheila says, although she noticed Daryl's flirtatious nature when she interviewed for the position of project manager at his firm she never imagined dating him or establishing an affair that would last over fifteen years. It began with subtle chats at the water cooler where they would bump into each other from time to time. The momentum grew as they began to enjoy each other's laughter while eating corporate lunches on staff appreciation day. The more instances the two were together the more relaxed and familiar they became with one another. Sheila felt honored when Daryl's superiors chose her to assist him with an upcoming project. To her delight, because she was fond of his personality and not because she felt any romantic attraction towards him, she committed to completing the assignment. The project was very intense and required both the two work in close proximity long hours a day. It never occurred to Sheila that Daryl was away from home more than usual and that his conversations began to shift from his wife and kids to her personal life. The long hours and more intimate conversations began to intrigue Sheila's curiosity; after all, she personally witnessed how Daryl treated his wife and children with love, affection and, care and she desired those things as well. Sheila's dilemma and internal struggle was her morals. She was taught that getting involved with a married man was totally off limits.

The project lasted months and now required the two to travel out of state together. Daryl understood that in order to get what he desired from Sheila he needed more alone time with her and because he was in charge of the project he could maneuver the working situation as needed to create the atmosphere necessary to accomplish his goals. I often share with men and women that if you do not find out what the objectives of others are, it may be difficult to ascertain the true sincerity of their motives. Sheila would find out after she allowed herself to be swayed by Daryl's charm (by the way charm is a deceptive spirit) attention to detail, affectionate ambitions and his conversation. His objective all along was to sleep with her. Daryl never desired to develop a long-term relationship with Sheila nor did he ever plan on leaving his family for her and that lesson cost Sheila her job, emotional distress and for a while physical ailments.

During the out of town visits, Daryl would have his assistant book a suite with two rooms so that he could have access to Sheila because he knew the more moments they had unsupervised by co-workers or his wife, would increase his chances of manipulating her. His plan worked to perfection as Sheila developed romantic feelings for Daryl and began sharing details that were more personal with him. When they finally had intercourse for the first time, she felt a sense of empowerment and that set in motion the events that would ensue.

Sheila stated, "*The sex was awesome because we had to be careful all the time, so when I would end up holding onto a cabinet in the office supply room while he penetrated me with quick thrusts during lunchtime, it would excite me like no other sex I'd ever had.*"

She admits it was tons of fun, until the "relationship" started moving from lust to emotion. "*I began behaving like a possessive child and that's when I knew it was time to let go*". However, Sheila continued, "*I knew many women who not only enjoyed lustful relationships with married men; they would take risks that I thought were simply immoral.*"

What did she think was immoral? -- Her list ranged from having sex in the married couple's bed to engaging in unprotected sex.

While it is easier to point the finger or lay blame on Sheila for her involvement with Daryl, I believe they shared the responsibility together for their choices but, Daryl because of the commitment he made to God and his wife.

According to a study conducted by the University of Louisville, many single women tend to engage in something the study referred to as "mate copying." In other words, such women tend to believe that if another woman is either after a man or with a man, there must be something he possesses that is worthy of pursuit.

Studies show that of the women polled who have admitted to having an affair with a married man; more than 45% did so because of their love of a challenge, drama, no strings or, the thrill of sin.

Many women also revealed that sex with attached men is usually incredible.

Women also replied that the following reasons also played a major part in their willing participation:

- More stimulating to be sneaky
- The intimacy is blistering
- Does not believe it will hurt anyone
- She justifies her actions with her expectations of men
- She needs to feel powerful
- The ring signifies experience
- It's all about competition
- It's carnal

In movies, the other woman typically depicted as a young, delusional being that just fell in love with the wrong person. The married man of course, is the user. He is the great deceiver who disregards his marital vows in the effort to fulfill his deep, sexual lust.

Although these stereotypes are popular, the truth is that the other woman may have a variety of agendas fueling her behavior. Depending on her age, social class and marital status, she might be carousing with another woman's man for several reasons other than love.

Why Married Men Date Single Women

While we are uncovered reasons, why a single woman may engage in a relationship with a married man the more opposing question would be why married men hook up with single women. I hope you are sitting down while you are reading this section because you will need a rest when you learn of the reasons why men say they have opted out of the sanctity of marriage to explore an adventure that most likely will end up a train wreck.

The Daily Beast website fathered an article by Jessica Ramirez, who stated that in her research for her book entitled "How to Keep Him from Cheating", statistics indicate that 50% of married men will cheat and at least 81% will not admit to doing so. Author Gary Neuman conducted a two-year case study of 100 men who had sexual affairs and 100 men who were faithful and shared his finding in his bestselling book "The Truth About Cheating: Why Men Stray and What You Can Do To Prevent It." Neuman, a marriage counselor for over twenty-years, discussed on the Oprah show that of the 9/11 firefighters who helped the wives of their fallen comrades ended up having affairs with them. He felt that example demonstrated or suggests that men make mistakes but, that their choices are not necessarily who they are. Neuman also says that people ascribe to the theory that men cheat for sex. His study revealed that only 8% of the adulterers polled stated that their sexual dissatisfaction was a primary contributor. Only 12% said the mistress was better looking or in better shape than their wives. The majority 48% stated that the affair was about an emotional disconnection and, feeling unappreciated was the number one reason for the disconnection.

We have been taught that men are sexual creatures. Arousal for men is simpler than for women. A percentage of married men will want sex and if they are not getting it from their spouse; they will seek it elsewhere. If the marriage has become stagnant in this area, the likelihood of an affair occurring is greater when either or both are not rooted in their faith with God. Sex is an integral component of marriage however; it should not be a leading component.

Men love the thrill of the hunt. This is because men created hunters like lions and once the chase is over, (i.e. he has captured the prey) men often times become lax. Therefore, when a man is experiencing issues at home rather, those issues are in the bedroom, financial cabinet, ego drawer or, emotional closet, a new chase may become eminent in his eye.

For men in particular, sex is their way of communicating their innermost feelings and when this is taken from the marriage, they may feel the need to obtain it from someone else. This thought process makes women outside of his marriage more attractive, single women because they are available and, married women because they understand.

Men love to be adored, respected and complimented. This makes him feel appreciated. A man enjoys affirmation and awards for the little things he does just as much as the enormous things he may do as well. When a married man has an encounter with a single woman, she may awaken the emotions he once felt for his wife but due to the challenges of marriage, may have suffered a silent death.

If you are a man who has ventured outside of your marriage and you truly wish to rebuild it you must immediately do the following:

- Take full responsibility for your actions
- Show remorse
- Be open for discussion about the affair(s)
- Seek professional and or spiritual assistance
- Commit to rebuilding
- Allow time for healing
- Forgive yourself
- Identify and eliminate problem areas (i.e. social media connections, phone numbers, emails, etc.)
- Create and execute a reconciliation plan

Marriage Not Included

When we buy certain items in stores or online they often come with a disclaimer that says, (Batteries Are Not Included). In the case of married people dating other married people, "Marriage is Not Included". Marriage is an institution that should be treated as such and although we make mistakes in life, we should look to rectify those mistakes versus issue concessions for why we continuously make the same type of choices. We only get stronger by assessing what we are doing and finding ways to make it better.

How Do We Grow From Here

We are often presented with problems in relationships but very few understand the dynamics of how to resolve them. If we want to improve our relationships, we must:

Appreciate The Assets: Men and women want to feel appreciated by their mate. Men generally want to give, and appreciation motivates them. Women adore men who show them gratitude for who they are and will reward them publicly and privately for doing so.

Be a Partner Not a Parent: You must treat your mate like an equal partner in the relationship versus being a parent. Complement one another on progression, think before you speak, and affirm often.

Create an Atmosphere for Quality Time: Life often gets in the way of relationships. If couples are not running to various events for the children, busy with church activities they are building careers at work. Something always presents itself as more important. You must create an atmosphere that invites quality time. Steal quiet moments away from the children and work to build moments that create lasting memories.

Actively Participate In Keeping It Spicy: Remember the artistry and dedication that you invested during the dating process. Communicate with your mate in a positive manner regarding the need to digest an innovative mindset as it relates to your relationship. Consistently compliment and encourage them to explore those fiery romantic dinners or secluded get-a-ways. Do not do what so many couples do which is, hold your breath and hope [the problem] goes away or the spice comes back.

Communicate! Communicate! Communicate!: Engage in at least four 45-minute periods of uninterrupted time a week where both turn off any outside distractions (i.e. phones, televisions, children) and spend time alone talking or playing board games or reading. Choose one night a week where you have a date night. It should be the same night every week. Get a babysitter ahead of time and during this time eliminate discussions about—money, business or the kids.

In order to restore your relationship after an affair you must be willing to deny yourself and shift your attention towards your spouse, after all, you had a great time exploring now you must commit to reconciling, restoring, and rebuilding your marriage. We are never going to be able to microwave a relationship. It is something that will require time and effort. We must focus on communicating effectively, being kind, showing appreciation, and implementing gestures that demonstrate our sincere love for our spouse continually.

Now and Later

Now and Laters is a brand of fruit-flavored taffy-like product which is organized into squares packaged in colorful paper. The candy is sold in packages containing three plastic-wrapped packs of six Now and Laters each, with plastic-wrapped pack containing a different flavor. "Hard 'N Fruity Now and Soft 'N Chewy Later," the slogan found on each square's wrapping, replaces "Eat Some Now. Save Some for Later."

I loved Now and Laters and would run back and forth to the candy store to satisfy my sweet tooth cravings. What we do now may affect us later. Building a solid foundation now will increase the prospects of having a healthy and fulfilling relationship later. You can apply this principle to any aspect of your life. If you sow seeds of manipulation, deceit, and corruption now, you may experience a horrid combustion of faulty wiring later. It is vitally important that we think about the now before we get to the later because not doing so could prove to be detrimental and hazardous to our character and integrity, which may affect us financially, professionally and socially.

PART SIX: HER MISSION

⏻ Power Point to Ponder

Life's choices will place you on many roads. You must make a conscience decision where the road will lead you before pressing the gas. Enjoy being single while preparing to be usable material for marriage but be sure to implement a stringent process when selecting your running mate. Own your choices and rectify your wrongs. Choose quality over quantity in addition, create and implement a reconciliation plan.

❓ Questions to Consider

Are you weighing the consequences and long-term effects of your current choices? Do you have a stringent vetting process for the running mate you're looking to choose?

💎 Jewel Tip

If you are more concerned with her assets…you are a liability!

POWER NOTES:

PART SEVEN

HER JEWELS

36 THE SUBSTITUTE

If you settle for the substitute, your classroom will never have the space to accommodate a fulltime teacher.

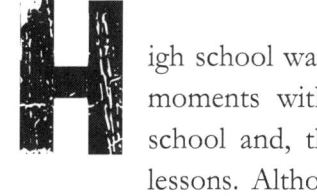

High school was a great time for me as I enjoyed precious moments with friends, the overall experience of high school and, the wonderful teachers that taught me life lessons. Although I had some great teachers, the days I arrived to class to find a substitute made the day go a bit easier. The substitute, unlike the teacher, did not have anything vested in the students therefore, often came across more understanding than sympathetic to our needs and an overall cooler adult. Most substitutes, when I was attending high school, were right out of college and searching for a permanent position.

Ironically, along my journey, I have been the substitute teacher that I loved when I was a student. I substituted a great deal in the Charlotte Mecklenburg and Union County North Carolina School Systems and enjoyed being the life of the classroom and engaging students to explore learning innovatively with my personality. I recall having an extreme crush on one of my substitute teachers during school and my vivid imagination led me to believe that we would actually have a relationship. I often wondered why I loved the substitute versus my teacher. As I grew older and was able to reflect, I realized the substitute provided something my teacher could not.

The substitute did not possess any more tutelage than my teacher did nor, did she present any innovative ways to learn because she provided a change of scenery. The substitute allowed us to forgo our educational responsibilities because she did not hold us accountable to our commitments. She infused herself within the classroom because she more than likely bore fear and wanted to make a good impression on the students. The substitute presented an escape. We could act out, be lazy and, waste time because the substitute was not going to disrupt our agenda and at times, would even participate.

We often wish to substitute our relationships with an alternative because it offers us an escape from reality, will not hold us accountable for our actions, enables us to go through the motions of life and, appeals to what we desire. However, living the substitute fantasy is only a temporary replacement; the teacher will eventually return.

We must rid our emotional database of corrupt files (our thinking) which convinces us that trouncing the original content in lieu of a superficial pipe dream will yield a greater reward. The teacher provides stability, a nurturing system, consistency and, a concrete plan.

When my mother passed away, I substituted my grief with work because it allowed me to escape from my reality. Pain prompted me to replace any thoughts of my mother or the numerous life issues I was dealing with at that time because processing the inevitable was unbearable. I substituted grief with busy work, hurt with humor, reality with fantasy because the truth of what I was dealing with I did not want to face. Many of us substitute love for the immediate gratification of its arch nemesis…lust.

We often confuse the two or fail to identify them properly and build relationships on one when we are seeking the other. We can equate this to going into an auto dealership in search of one vehicle only to settle for another because the salesperson convinces you that the vehicle you want is out of your reach. Trained sales representatives talk you out of your desires because of what may await them on the back end of the deal. I am not suggesting that you engross yourself in debt by attempting to purchase things you cannot viably afford I am challenging you to pursue the things you desire knowing what you want and properly aligning yourself with the tools necessary to attain those things. In your relationship you must cease to settle for one-nightstands and exotic thrills when in your heart you desire to become someone's husband or wife.

Getting Everything You Need

We often convince ourselves that because of our involvement with someone who only satisfies a small percentage of our needs. We are actually getting all we need. When you are involved in a relationship that allows for partial commitment from your partner, you deprive yourself from a fruitful and fulfilling relationship. I have heard many stories of men and women settling for mates that devote little time, energy or, effort to the relationship but perform exceptionally on occasion. Those far and in between moments suffice for the other 90% of the time. They are emotionally, physically and, romantically absent according to the preprogrammed mindset of their spouses. This notion comes as a shock to many because it seems that a fruitful relationship is unattainable for the mate seeking one. This is very true. In order to get everything you need from your relationship you must first understand what it is you want. Secondly, know your worth to the relationship. Understand what you deserve as a man or woman who has set a standard for what you will allow in your life. Finally, project the things that you wish to attract in your relationship and place an expectation on the mate you interview for the position to fulfill those expectations.

I have a saying, "If you choke your potential before it has an opportunity to become a possibility you will never reach your destiny." If you continuously settle for the substitute, your classroom will never have the space to accommodate a fulltime teacher.

JUST AN OPTION NOT A PRIORITY

37

Options are given…Priority is taken.

Nowadays, almost every business entity is offering a bundle of options to their services, bombarding consumers with selections to add this and alter that. I am concerned that companies are flooding us with options rather than giving us what we need.

Mobile carrier providers are excellent at giving you a bunch of options that are not priority. I recall when my wife and I were experiencing a high phone bill monthly and could not figure out why the bill seemed to continue to rise when the representative confidently assured me that we were getting the best deal possible. She suggested a new plan that would lower our bill. I must have spoken to several customer service operators over several years to attempt to resolve this ongoing issue and one day my wife came to me and said the bill was ridiculously out of hand and something needed to be done immediately. Of course, hearing this would make any man scammer to make something happen. It reminded me of the scene in the epic movie starring Denzel Washington, Robert

Duvall, Anne Heche, Ray Liotta and Kimberly Elise entitled "John Q".

The film follows John Quincy Archibald (Denzel Washington), a father and husband whose son is diagnosed with an enlarged heart and then finds out he cannot receive a transplant because HMO insurance will not cover it. His wife, played by Kimberly Elise, distraught by the tragedy and suffering from extreme pressure urges her husband to do something. He decides to take a hospital full of patient's hostage until the hospital puts his son's name on the recipient's list. My wife's sentiments regarding our phone bill were not as extreme but nevertheless, her tone was poignant and I knew something needed to change right away.

I phoned my mobile carrier again and when the representative asked what she could do for me I said, "I need to prioritize my bill and eliminate options". What I learned about the structure of my bill was amazing. I had a data plan but if all I needed was to talk and text on my phone it was not necessary to have the data plan and it was costing us extra money for this option.

Many of you have either been someone's option versus a priority or vice versa. My service provider initially gave me the notion that I needed the data plan for basic operation and on several occasions, reiterated this by training its representatives to issue subtle impressions of information pushing the data plan to its customers. In actuality, what I needed did not require a data plan at all. The phone was fully operable to make calls and text. As long as I did not access the internet, Facebook, Twitter or any other application that used the data line, I could lower my monthly phone bill by over $100 dollars.

Men and women manipulate each other just as mobile service providers. They are motivated to garner as much from you as possible, without committing "the extra." My ignorance caused me to overpay for years because I did not ask the proper questions .The day I decided that my financial destiny was top priority I no longer opted to be an option to my phone provider. I suffered through many conversations with men and women who allowed their mates and spouses to continue making them an option versus a priority. This was due in part because they lacked either the power to ask the hard questions or, the will to start over because familiarity had a bigger grasp on their hearts than the reality of being a meager option.

Identifying what or who is priority or an option is the key to developing a long-term relationship of substance. If you are someone who enjoys being the center of attention but your mate seemingly finds alternative subjects to entertain, chances are you are in the option category. If you are someone who's involved with a mate who is committed to another, chances are you are the option versus the priority. If you do not believe me conduct a quick study of your present position and I will gladly wait for you to email me the results. You know you are an option when your mate consistently cancels dates or long-standing appointments for last minute pleasures such as an outing with the girls or a ball game with the guys.

Convenience Cushion

Do you want to avoid becoming the dreadful "convenience cushion?" Of course, and yes, it is an adventure. Both men and women spend countless hours dating, in an attempt to cycle through the fluff of potential suitors. Unfortunately, these same men and women find themselves to be expediency when they are longing to become the primary. You can identify those who are seeking stability and a long-term commitment, opposed to those who are merely in search of a consolation selection if you pay close attention to the verbal and nonverbal cues.

38 DIAMOND MINE OR CITY DUMP?

What one trash another will value...you must determine which is which!

What is the difference between a diamond mine and a city dump? Many would argue the contents found within its grounds and that prognosis would be correct. What you find at one you will not necessarily find at the other, although there are exceptions to the rule. There are a limited number of commercially viable diamond mines currently operating in the world. In order to understand my analogy of how a city dump and diamond mine relate to you and relationships I must break down the terms used. When we look at the definition of the word mining what comes to mind? Mining is the extraction (removal) of minerals and metals from the earth. A diamond is renowned as a material with superlative physical qualities, most of which originate from the strong covalent bonding between its atoms. In particular, a diamond has the highest hardness and thermal conductivity of any bulk material. Diamonds have remarkable optical characteristics. Because of its extremely rigid lattice, very few types of impurities can contaminate it. Therefore, we would gather that a diamond mine in reference to my text is the extracting of something with superlative physical qualities, supreme value and remarkable optical characteristics.

A landfill site (also known as a city dump) is a site for the disposal of waste materials by burial and is the oldest form of waste treatment. Throughout history, landfills have been the most common method of organizing waste disposal and remain so in many places around the world today.

Landfills may include internal waste disposal sites (where a producer of waste carries out their own waste disposal at the place of production) as well as sites used by many producers. Landfills are also used for waste management such as the temporary storage, consolidation and, transfer or processing of waste material (sorting, treatment, or recycling).

A landfill may also refer to ground that has been filled in with rocks instead of waste materials so that it can be used for a specific purpose such as for building houses.

When we are in search of a mate who will become our wife, we must be extremely careful of where we search for her and furthermore, what type of woman she is. While it is seemingly obvious to many that if we were to look at my comparison, we would think most men would search for a woman in a diamond mine versus a city dump. Truth is, there are many jewels (women) found in various locations. However, taking a jewel from a city dump to a diamond mine mentality could prove challenging. While jewels are born in diamond mines, they may be created in a city dump.

I grew up in the inner city housing projects of Atlanta but the inner city never resided in me. I wanted more out of life than what my circumstances presented and therefore, never adopted the mentality that many of my childhood friends adopted. For many of my peers the inner city was the pinnacle of their young lives. They never envisioned accomplishing more than their parents, being more than a blue-collar worker or, a drug dealer. The opportunities were endless; had they applied themselves nothing was impossible.

If you are someone with a big vision and your mate has small thinking, you may encounter a great deal of resistance. Grasp this: It is not that your mate wants less out of life; but no one taught them how to get more from life. You must be prepared to exercise great patience or become a great teacher. The progress of your relationship will hinge on your ability to adapt. We have all heard the term "One man's trash is another man's treasure" and this statement could very well be your reality. What transforms trash into treasure is the viewpoint of the treasure hunter. Your mate or potential mate may have experienced neglect in areas of proper care. Her previous mate may have seen the task of teaching or cultivating a headache and lost interest in pursuing. I have heard many stories of someone selling something they found worthless only to learn that it possessed great value.

Remember it is not as important where you find your mate as it is what you do with the mate you find. Whether you meet them at work, church or, a mall enter into the relationship with a notion to polish whatever you discover at the diamond mine or the city dump. You may not be the lifetime owner of what you discover but like a great collector you will prepare the findings for whoever finds them later.

39 CYCLE OF ACCEPTANCE

A repetitive behavior of neglect will force you to accept the untimely outcome of defeat versus fighting for victory.

I believe the spouse's quest to fulfill our needs isn't what drives men & women to seek relationship refreshments elsewhere is a personal choice to fulfill selfish desires...and for some men sex was not what initially allowed him to entertain her. She did what Delilah did...she grabbed his vulnerable sex organ...his eyes, and lured him into her passionate web by simply filling the holes in his need for assurance. Studies show in over 65% of marital affairs the initial entrance is initiated by an innocent dialogue that takes place in a comfortable environment inviting a number of influential possibilities.

Many of us accept certain behaviors our mate or potential mate possesses and deem the acceptance forthcoming. Women welcome boyfriends and husbands back after learning of infidelity and other improprieties without those men having any brokenness about their actions. When we are truly regretful of any action or decision we make that affects the lives of others, there is some sort of remorse that speaks well beyond words.

Not Sorry Just Apologetic

We often say we are sorry but are merely apologetic for being exposed. There is a huge difference between admission of guilt and sincere repentance. An apology is a formal admission of wrongdoing. It may or may not be heartfelt. Admission of guilt says, at times I am regretful that you found out but I have no plans of changing the very actions that have hurt you because it is my objective to continue seeking my own desires. On the other hand, saying "I am sorry" is a truer admission of regret and is very heartfelt. A sincere repentance demonstrates through the actions of change that it is dutifully remorseful in the shame and embarrassment it has caused those it loves and sincerely cares for and furthermore, will relinquish any self-observant behavior detrimental to the building or upkeep of the relationship in which it is grateful to be involved.

I can assure you that in any relationship you will encounter one or both of these after a while and should be able to identify them properly. To assist you with a guide I have listed the characteristics of both below:

Apologetic

- Not emotionally attached towards a situation
- Excuses for actions
- More political
- Feeds selfish desires
- Deflects responsibility of actions Abuses the situation
- Avoids dealing with consequences

Remorseful

- Sympathetic towards a situation
- Honest feelings of guilt
- More personal
- Causes deep reflection
- Accepts responsibility of actions
- Protects the situation from further injury
- Deals with Consequences

When you accept the wrongful behavior of your spouse continually, you enable and subject yourself to a cycle of acceptance of this type of behavior and devalue the relationship greatly. We must assess every situation in our relationship while maintaining love and forgiveness. We must also understand that if someone merely apologizes each time they are exposed without attempting to correct their behavior; – you may be involved in a toxic relationship.

A cycle of acceptance could also equate to you accepting any form of abuse from your spouse. I have watched numerous reality television programs with men and women who accept verbal, mental and physical abuse from their spouse or significant other and it is unacceptable. You should not subject yourself to any form of abuse, for it tears down the core fibers of any relationship and exposes insecurity.

Today understand that you are more valuable than the abuse or excuses your mate continues to provide and, if you persist in allowing the behavior, you are diminishing your value.

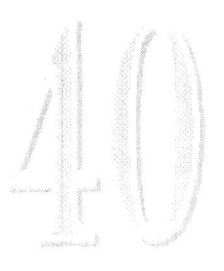

I'M NOT READY 40

Being prepared is not comparable to being ready. You may be ready for something that you are not dutifully prepared for.

Life often times will throw us curves balls so illusive that we cannot hit the pitches. What matters in life is not how many pitches it throws, but that you continue to stay in the batter's box swinging at the pitches. Tragedy or trauma will show up in our lives like an unwanted houseguest and we are not sure how long it plans to stay. I recall after losing my mother and while in the process of a very bad relationship breakup, I felt as if I was not ready to face all that was ahead for me. The pain of facing life without my best friend, adapting to my new business venture and tackling the devastation of a failed marriage was not what I expected to confront when I envisioned my life unfolding. I began writing again and what came out of my being was exhilarating and necessary. I realized at that moment that I was not ready for what was ahead for me and this is how I felt.

I am not ready to face the wiles
Of this day
I'm not ready but you know I won't say.

I'm not ready
And I can't hide,
I wasn't ready so I lied.
I'm not ready for the anguish
And strain this divorce will bring,
But I have to take it!
I wasn't ready for mama to go to glory
But I have to face it.

I'm not ready for the smoke screens
This world will shoot me
Nor am I ready for the cold shoulders
It will bare
I'm not ready to be ready
And some days I really don't care.

I'm not ready
To be successful for fear of the
problems it will bring my way,
I'm not ready
For tomorrow because
I can't deal with the realities of today.

I don't know how long it will take
To break my silence or heal my heart.
I won't understand my mold nor the direction
Of my soul,
I can only tell you it's hard keeping
This life that's so rocky and fragile steady
And even harder realizing that
When the record stops playing and the lights go dim
I will be faced with decisions of yesterday

And that alone makes me believe that I Am **NOT READY**!!!

When life deals us an uncertain hand it makes it difficult at times to adequately prepare for what is in store when we are not sure what to expect. I once heard a story about a man who was captured behind enemy lines and was sentenced to be killed or given another option. The captain said to the man "Tomorrow morning at six o'clock you can face the firing range or go out this door", the man asked, "What's outside the door?" the captain replied "no one knows, all we can tell you is just unknown horrors". The man thought for a moment and the next morning he selected the firing range. After the shots rang out the captain's secretary said, "What is beyond that door?" the captain replied, freedom but very few people would select it because it is unknown".

We often shy away from business ventures, career opportunities or marriage because of the unknown. Many have witnessed others experience hardship in marriage and decide that the fate of others may very well be their own and live a life of uncertainty moving from relationship to unfulfilled relationship.

Preparing for life, marriage or building a healthy relationship will be an ongoing process that will continue to evolve with time. You must not grow weary in your well doing because if you faint not the bible says you will reap a just reward.

GOOD ENOUGH TO BE THE ROOMMATE

41

For the LORD will be your confidence and will keep your foot from being snared. Proverbs 3:26

Going to college was a dream of mine initially but turned into a nightmare soon after my arrival, at least in my dorm. I wasn't sure if the dorm monitor got a hold of my high school transcript and decided that I needed a roommate who would challenge my study habits or, if a hologram of Santa Claus told them I had been naughty. I spent most of my life in a room of my own and aside from the camping trips we took as Royal Ambassadors at my church, I'd never had a roommate.

The first few weeks were blissful as in any new relationship because everyone had a protective shield up attempting to impress the other. But soon after the representatives left, it became apparent that my roommate and I were not meant to be together. We were 18-year-old young men who had lived in our parent's homes with no responsibilities. On top of that, we had to learn to live with strangers. My first roommate did not last the semester and he requested reassignment. I had one other roommate during my first year and then another one part of summer school. I came to the alarming discovery that a roommate was too much work and the requirements necessary to maintain one was not on my to-do-list.

College birthed some great moments and aside from the roommate fiasco, I truly had some memorable experiences. One of the most humbling experiences came the beginning of my sophomore year. I spent the previous summer working out to make tryouts for the football team at North Carolina State University. However, after not putting in as much work with my academics as I did my athletics, I had to return to complete the year and improve my grades. The football coach at my school felt that my ambitions to play for a larger school prompted me to shun tryouts for his team and therefore, refused to allow me on the team. After this devastating news, I wallowed in self-pity for a moment and one day, on my way from class, a group of students approached me about me applying my athletic skills on their flag football team.

It puzzled me that with all of my accolades and promise as a prep-football player in high school and my tenacity in college why the coach would not allow me on the team yet, a group of ambitious, passionate students to whom I was a foreigner were excited to draft me to their team.

That scenario taught me a great deal about relationships and the expectations that lie within them. I determined that the people who I roomed with were indeed good people and maybe even great roommates but, for someone else,-not me. Often in life, we meet individuals who feel that we are great men but we are only good enough for certain aspects of a relationship with them, either personal or professional and, proceed with building the relationship accordingly while we are looking for permanent suitors or long-term houseguests.

If you are in search of a monogamous relationship that will eventually develop into an engagement and marriage, you must lay the foundation to a home that will build closets for two versus merely sharing the space of one.

If your mate only values your portion of the relationship just above you being a boy-toy or an in-house sex slave, there is a serious disconnect with expectations. Understanding that you add more value to a relationship than what your mate may see is the key to forming relationships that are more suitable for you long-term. I realized in college that I was a better person to visit than to have as a roommate. You must decide what type of individual you want to be in the relationship and communicate that expectation to your mate.

Failing to understand what you want or how your mate has categorized you will place you in a position that may either undervalue your contribution to the relationship or cause you to experience lack within the relationship.

If you desire to be more than just a boyfriend or girlfriend, you must project what you expect and make it very clear what you will tolerate. If not, you could spend five to ten years simply being someone's roommate because they do not value you as anything more.

42 YOU WANT TO MATTER

And those he predestined, he also called; those he called, he also justified; those he justified, he also glorified. What, then, shall we say in response to this? If God is for us, who can be against us?
Romans 8:30-31

Society has painted a sordid picture of what is important and what is not, who matters and who doesn't, what's hot and what's not to a point that many of us are programmed to believe that if we don't fit the description, we are not relevant. This alarming statistic concerns me deeply.

The above scripture reminds me that when God created us he made sure that we understood how much we mattered to him. He says that those whom he called he has also justified. I often wonder why so many are starving for attention. Why are so many men and women hungry for fame and what happened to those individuals to cause such a drive to be seen, heard or a need to feel wanted?

I have seen postings on social media sites such as Twitter and Facebook, watched disturbing videos on YouTube and the detestable

World Star Hip-Hop (and I say this because it appears that they do not have a moral standard for what they will allow on their site). It has beckoned me to propose the obscure question, "Why do people view themselves as valueless"?

Reading and studying the book of Genesis in the bible somewhat answered my question. Scripture says in Genesis 2:7 (New Living Translation) *Then the LORD God formed the man from the dust of the ground. He breathed the breath of life into the man's nostrils, and the man became a living person.* "From the dust of the ground" implies that there is nothing fancy about the chemical elements making up our bodies. The body is a lifeless shell until God brings it alive with his "breath of life." When God removes his life-giving breath, our bodies return to dust. Therefore, our life and worth come from God's Spirit. That says to me that without us operating in God's spirit, we will often feel inadequate searching for validation through relationships, our mates, materialistic things, employment/church positions and titles, social statuses, the amount of money in our bank accounts or, who we are associated with. In reality, our worth comes from the God of the universe, who chooses to give us the mysterious and miraculous gift of life.

"Attempting to matter to someone who has repeatedly demonstrated that you, your concerns or cares aren't important to them is like a kidnapper convincing the kidnapped to forget the abduction and not press charges once he's been cornered by authorities"-Mo Stegall

---

This mindset or acts of disobedience are what push us toward self-gratification and acceptance. If you do not believe me, dive a bit deeper into the biblical story of "The Tower of Babel", the bible says in Genesis 11:1-9

At one time all the people of the world spoke the same language and used the same words. As the people migrated to the east, they found a plain in the land of Babylonia and settled there.

They began saying to each other, "Let's make bricks and harden them with fire." (In this region, bricks were used instead of stone, and tar was used for mortar.) Then they said, "Come, let's build a great city for ourselves with a tower that reaches into the sky. This will make us famous and keep us from being scattered all over the world."

But the Lord came down to look at the city and the tower the people were building. "Look!" he said. "The people are united, and they all speak the same language. After this, nothing they set out to do will be impossible for them! Come, let's go down and confuse the people with different languages. Then they won't be able to understand each other."

In that way, the Lord scattered them all over the world, and they stopped building the city. That is why the city was called Babel, because that is where the Lord confused the people with different languages. In this way he scattered them all over the world.

The tower of Babel was a great human achievement, a wonder of the world. However, it was a monument to the people themselves rather than to God. We may build monuments to ourselves (expensive clothes, big house, fancy cars, important jobs, etc.) to call attention to our achievements. We may feel these things add value to our lives equating our self worth or identifying who we are but they do not. We will be who we are regardless if we accumulated any of

those possessions and they do not make us yet, they are markings of achievements that we are given the ability to attain.

In order for us to add value to any relationship we develop be it personal or professional, we must first understand and know our worth. I talked about this in my bestselling empowerment guide "Against All Odds I Can Be: 10 Steps To Revolutionize Your Destiny" in chapter one. Failing to discover what you are individually worth prior to engaging in any type of relationship may place you at a disadvantage and render you dependent upon the relationship to define your worth.

Co-Dependency

People across the globe define who they are based upon a number of superficial non-merited factors such as where they work, what they drive, how much money they have or their position in a church. However, our identity is based upon our character and integrity.

Character, speaks to our moral or ethical quality. Some of us are like the roles given to Hollywood actors and we are waltzing through life portraying a fictional character. It's identified in today's society as we see more and more people looking to become famous but possess no apparent talent.

When a woman views a man, she should be able to rest knowing that he has character and integrity. His character is what he displays when others are looking but his integrity is what he displays when no one is around. He has such a high standard for himself that he desires to be the same man privately as he is publicly.

I once worked for a large investment firm and at times, I would often work in a room with millions of dollars. Because I was young, I would daydream about actually possessing the amount of money I saw on the slips of paper in my hand. As immature as I was then, I had enough integrity to dream only without any other thoughts of walking out of the building attempting to take something that did not belong to me.

Your mate must be able to trust that you are the person you present to them when they are not around. I have seen a number of men who pretend to have riches or high positions in order to impress a woman, only to have her discover later that the presentation was a fraud. I often asked myself why he felt as if he needed to present someone other than who he truly was and, I only needed to look at myself to gather an answer.

Growing up in public housing with little resources or finances caused me to drift at times into a fantasy world that did not exist. My self-esteem was very low because I defined who I was by what I did not have, so as I grew older I became increasingly concerned with image and appearances. I wanted to feel wanted and when I saw others buying nice things, driving nice cars and living in nice homes I believed that if I had those things people would be more inclined to like me. The reality of my life caused me to feel empty and therefore, during my earlier years of adolescence I began to rebel against my mother because I wanted to matter to a culture of people who could care less if I existed. What life has taught me since those times and as I observe the behavior of others is we all want to be significant to something or someone. When we feel empty, it causes us to react, meaning we may do things without viewing the consequences of our actions thoroughly.

Tale of the Tiger

When the news broke about Tiger Woods exploitations, many of the women who willingly participated in the egregious acts of infidelity knowing that he was a married man came forward, some even holding press conferences and receiving book deals in return. I am not excusing Tiger's behavior, but we condemned him while many celebrated the women. Mainstream media acted as if those women were coerced into the relationship and painted them as victims. Many argued that those women not only willingly participated with full knowledge of the ramifications that may ensue if the secret was uncovered but, profited from their relationship with Tiger.

No matter how you shake these types of situations, nothing good comes of it because it has hurt a number of people involved but most importantly, his wife, kids and, his family. Some of the women involved did not want their affair to go public, while others paraded themselves in the public eye as Tiger's innocent victims. The latter women enlisted attorneys in order to capitalize on the ordeal.

> *Just because everyone does not know who you are does not make you nobody…it simply means others may be more popular than you are.*

Aiming to be relevant in a relationship that does not invite you to do so is somewhat relationship suicide. Tiger Woods seemingly did not care about most, if not all, of the women he had sexual relations with and, could have possibly used them to satisfy his sexual appetite. The women did not respect themselves or care about him because they allowed themselves to be reduced to a secret sex slave. They more than likely sought validation from someone the world revered as important and found it necessary to indulge in the relationship because of how it made them feel to seemingly be chosen by Woods. I say seemingly because it was evident by his marriage to Elin that those women were not priority and because everything was done in secrecy demonstrates his value of them.

Our importance to someone must be validated through his or her care for us, the ongoing demonstration of love, concern and, improvement to us personally and professionally. The growth of two individuals should not prompt one to degrade, belittle or, disrespect himself in order to please the other.

Healthy relationships are based upon the manner in which each person contributes to the construction and maintenance of one another. If repairs or renovations are necessary to maintain the edifice (relationship), we must invest in the upkeep or we will be a factor in its demolition.

43 BECOMING THE TREASURE HUNTER

The value of a woman is not defined by the price tag attached to her shoes or clothes or the intimate moments she discloses, but by what she adds to you with her presence.

When you think of treasure hunting one would automatically think of someone exhausting themselves over a rumored buried fortune or unbelievable riches in the northwest desert where countless prosperous dynasties have flourished and fallen. In recent times, the early stages of the development of archaeology included a significant aspect of treasure hunting Heinrich Schliemann's excavations at Troy, and later at Mycenae, both turned up significant finds of golden artifacts. Early work in Egyptology also included a similar motive.

I wanted you to get a visual image of what becoming a treasure hunter would entail so I have included a few facts. More recently, most serious treasure hunters have started working underwater, where modern technology allows access to wrecks containing valuables that were previously inaccessible. Starting with the diving suit, and moving on through Scuba and later to ROVs, each new generation of technology has made more wrecks accessible. Many of these wrecks have resulted in the treasure salvage of many fascinating artifacts from Spanish treasure fleets as well as many others. Treasure hunters such as Capt. Martin Bayerle who located the shipwreck of RMS Republic in 1981, or Ponce de Leon who searched the new world for gold and the Fountain of Youth, and Heinrich Schliemann a grocer turned treasure hunter, considered father of historical archaeology who discovered the lost city of Troy.

As men we are designed to be hunters, many of us may have never gone fishing or hunted game with our fathers but we were designed to be hunters. When I think of hunting, I am reminded of how a hunter prepares to hunt his target. Hunting is considered a sport and for years men have hunted women for various reasons. Not all are reasons he would discuss with his pastor but, nonetheless, in his hunting he has made some alarming discoveries about his prey. The question is what are we hunting? I believe in order to become efficient hunters we must be able to both define and understand what treasures we are pursuing.

According to Wikipedia, a treasure is described as a concentration of riches, often one which is considered lost or forgotten until being rediscovered. Women are designed to be desired and found. **Proverbs 18:22** backs this theory as it states, *"The man who finds a wife finds a treasure, and he receives favor from the LORD."(NLT)* As hunters, you must delicately decipher your prey and pursue it with a delightful and daring chase. Finding the treasure could be a mystery in itself and many of you may wonder what is truly required to become a treasure hunter.

Hunting for treasure sounds romantic and thrilling, like something out of a romantic action movie and it can be all of that.

However, it also involves planning and hard work. Pinpointing the treasure's location is assignment number one, since you rarely will have a map marked with a big X to guide you. You must strongly consider the financial aspect of being able to provide for the woman you are pursuing if you want to become a treasure hunter. You will need to be able to adequately provide for her financially, emotionally, and spiritually.

Seek wise counsel in your quest to become a successful treasure hunter. Few people ever achieve anything great all by themselves. If you do not have the necessary detective skills to seek out valuables, find someone who does. It will improve your chances of success if you seek someone with wise counsel who can assist you with analyzing information.

Most men are taught as young boys that hunting multiple targets is the rite of passage to becoming a "Real Man" and depending on the type of treasure, you want to find, there are expeditions going out all over the world that will provide a chance to gain experience. Many would say the more experiences you have with educational, exploring types of trips, the better. I believe that exploring is good because it will assist you in learning the value between genuine treasures and priceless metal but frivolous hunting with no long-term objective of discovering a jewel you can marvel over and one that appreciates you as well is a hazardous suicide mission.

To become an effective treasure hunter you must possess the following:

Gear

I know, you think that you have it all figured out and do not necessarily need assistance but I beg to differ! In order to be a hunter who actually hunts and finds treasure versus the finds you may have found in recent years you will need the proper gear. A football player in the National Football League would not go onto the field wearing a hockey mask and soccer shorts, so you should not go on your journey of finding your jewel of a woman with the wrong tools. We are taught that all you need is "game" to get a woman; well I am here to notify you like the county sheriff during an eviction that you have been misinformed. Game is as it sounds and I define as a form of manipulation and deceit. I believe it conjures a man to believe the lies he or others may have told him and allows him to present that representative I spoke of earlier and not his identity. Your gear will include a camera, two-way radio, headlamp, wool socks, and raingear.

- **Camera**- not a physical camera but a mental image of the woman you will need versus the one that you desire. Need implies that she will assist you in accomplishing your goals long-term versus satisfying a temporary desire.
- **Two-way Radio**-you will need to occupy the ability to communicate and listen. Simply talking without intently listening will cause chaos in your home and disable your ability to communicate effectively with the jewel you will find.
- **Headlamp**- you must be able to see where you are going to obtain the relationship you desire but also be able to maneuver through the dark moments once you have the mate you seek. A headlamp does two things, it shows you were you are and guides you to where you need to be.
- **Wool Socks**- you will have moments where your footing will seem unsure, wool socks (solid footing) will allow you to stand firm on your goals and beliefs while keeping you warm during the winter moments of your relationship.
- **Raingear**- nothing is more irritating and frustrating than being caught out in a rainstorm without a raincoat or poncho. You will need raingear to protect you from the rainstorms that many experience in relationships.

Being Physically Fit

This might seem like common sense, but too many people ignore it. How fit are you? Be honest now. Can you run without keeling over? Can you climb a long rope? Can you do a pull up? How strong are you? Many physical trainers will ask these questions before engaging in an extreme workout but you must ask yourself on your quest to finding the jewel you desire are you physically fit to stay the course and give chase. Relationships are exhausting and you must be physically in shape to continue running to locate the treasure that you seek regardless of the conditions presented.

Being Psychologically Fit

Are you psychologically capable of going on long and strenuous hunting expeditions? Are you comfortable with tight, enclosed spaces? How well do you handle high stress situations? A psychologist may ask these questions. A number of things you will encounter during your relationships either personal or professional will require you to be psychologically fit to handle various situations. Mental toughness is a state of mind that says *"Losing Is Simply Not An Option"* so you must continue the journey until you have found or rediscovered the lost treasure.

Knowledge

Proverbs 1:20 says *"Wisdom crieth without; she uttereth her voice in the streets: She crieth in the chief place of concourse, in the openings of the gates: in the city she uttereth her words, saying How long, ye simple ones, will ye love simplicity? and the scorners delight in their scorning, and fools hate knowledge?"*

- Expanding your reach and your search will begin with you seeking and gaining wisdom and knowledge. It is God's desire to give you the foresight and insight to be successful in every aspect of your life. The scriptures below can be used as a starting point.

- *I will certainly give you the wisdom and knowledge you requested. But I will also give you wealth, riches, and fame such as no other king has had before you or will ever have in the future!* **2Chronicles 1:12** *Ask and it will be given to you; seek and you will find; knock and the door will be opened to you.* **Matthew 7:7**

THE JEWEL EXPERT 44

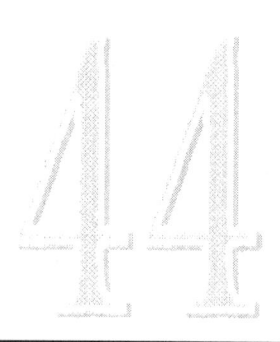

A true expert understands his limit while celebrating his strengths. He values his time and that of others and dedicates himself to constantly improving.

I love the scripture in Matthew 7:7 that says, **"Ask and it will be given to you; seek and you will find; knock and the door will be opened to you"** because it is something about both knowing if I seek or go after something I have a strong chance of both finding and getting it. Many men and women across the globe are aimlessly longing for a companion who will love them, appreciate them, adorn, respect and grow old with them; you are no different from any of them. I believe the issue is not that there is a low surplus of available men and women, it is that we have no idea what we are expected to find while on our scavenger hunt.

One of the questions I receive ongoing is "What is a **Jewel Expert?**" A **Jewel Expert** is a man who is a master at identifying gems. He takes his time to study the vernacular of a woman, her mind and spirit versus primarily focusing on her precious commodities. He listens with intent to empower versus tear her down...he's not perfect but he understands her worth and will work at his short-comings because he realizes she is a one of a kind and doesn't treat her like she is another piece of costume jewelry. He is equipped and insured, has been thoroughly trained to handle high-pressure situations, delicate and sensitive materials and knows how to transport them efficiently. A **Jewel Expert** is a man who appreciates the creation of women because he had a dynamic, loving and fulfilling relationship with his mother and therefore values his relationship with the woman he may identify as his friend, girlfriend, fiancé or wife.

License & Credentials

In various countries it is primary to obtain a license and proper credentials if you wish to operate a motor vehicle legally, sell real-estate or carry a firearms so why should dating be any different? After all, we are handling treasured cargo and engaging in high profile relationships with sensitive materials disclosed that could be potentially harmful if fallen into the wrong hands. For many years, I have had a fondness of the government agencies that serve and protect or protect and serve, in particular the United States Secret Service.

The United States Secret Service is a federal law enforcement agency with headquarters in Washington, D.C., and more than 150 offices throughout the United States and abroad. The Secret Service established in 1865, solely to suppress the counterfeiting of U.S. currency. Today, the agency is mandated by Congress to carry out dual missions: to uphold the tradition of excellence in its investigative and protective mission through a dedicated, highly trained, diverse, partner-oriented workforce that employs progressive technology and promotes professionalism. It is also the agency's mission to safeguard the nation's financial infrastructure and payment systems to preserve the integrity of the economy, and to protect national leaders, visiting heads of state and government, designated sites and National Special Security Events.

What is intriguing about the agency is its extensive and scrupulous training program. If you have a desire to become a secret service agent you must complete a 10-week course. This course is somewhat of an orientation to the agency and covers various areas and upon completion. You then enter a 17-week Special Agent Training Course which focuses on specific Secret Service policies and procedures associated with the dual responsibilities of investigation and protection.

People often engage in relationships without any prerequisite requirements and frequently speculate the cause of those relationships tapering off or spiraling downward. In order to become a Jewel Expert you must complete the training program and receive the proper license and credentials.

To become the man she essentially desires will require extensive training in marksmanship, control tactics, water survival skills and physical fitness.

Marksmanship: An expert shooter is a person who is skilled in precision, or a sharpshooter using projectile weapons to shoot at long-range targets. You must be able to hit the mark precisely understanding what the target is during an argument or disagreement and aiming for the solution versus prolonging the mislaid issue.

Control Tactics: You must be able to manage compliant and non-compliant concerns within your relationship by developing tactics and techniques that will assist you in discerning and disarming hostile components and manipulative devices that may cause tension. It will also assist you with maintaining a level head during fiery combat and keep your emotions intact.

Water Survival Skills: The best of swimmers have drowned in troubled waters. You must be able to tread the waves of problematic conditions and safely carry the relationship to the shore of solutions.

Physical Fitness: Have you ever attempted to run a marathon without training properly? I can tell you that paramedics would be summoned to assist you if you attempted to do so. To Successfully endure the course of any relationship, you must be in shape to handle the various terrains that you will have to travel to build trust, consistency and continuity. A trainer understands the process of training the mind to respond to the physical demands that the body issues and the methods necessary to get both components into shape. You must properly train yourself to respond to the demands of growing a healthy, productive and fruitful relationship. A distance runner who consistently wins races grasp that his ability to run alone isn't enough to win yet, it is how he conditions himself that will allow him to pace himself accordingly to distribute the proper amount of speed and power at the precise moment to outrun his opponents. Your ability to identify the appropriate times to proceed or discontinue will position you to become the Jewel Expert many women essentially need.

When Does a Gem Become a Jewel?

When does a gem actually become a jewel? Before we can adequately answer the question, we must first identify or define what a gem is.

A **gemstone** or **gem** is a piece of mineral, which, in cut and polished form, is used to make jewelry or other adornments. Most gemstones are hard, but some soft minerals are used in jewelry because of their luster or other physical properties that have aesthetic value. Scientists say that a gem becomes a jewel when it is cut, polished or used in jewelry

For thousands of years humans have been adorning themselves with gems and jewels to stand out and wow an audience. In the form of necklaces, rings, pendants, or bracelets, the precious and rare gems – mounted on jewelry – have long since become one of the favored ways to express just how much wealth one has.

In conjunction with or synonymous to gems, jewels and jewelry men since the beginning of time have done the same with women. I am not suggesting or portraying women as pieces of property or mere accessories. I am making the comparing contrast that as individuals adorn themselves with necklaces, bracelets, pendants, etc. to display their affection towards those material belongings so should men view the significance of the woman that he seeks as something precious and valuable enough to express his love and adoration for her publicly as people does with their jewelry.

Characteristics and Classification

Again, the burgeoning question is when does a gem become a jewel? Before we can proceed, we must learn the characteristics and classification of gemstones.

The traditional classification in the West, which goes back to the Ancient Greeks, begins with a distinction between precious and semi-precious stones; similar distinctions made in other cultures. In modern usage, the precious stones are diamond, ruby, sapphire and emerald, with all other gemstones classified as semi-precious. This distinction reflects the rarity of the respective stones in ancient times, as well as their quality. All are translucent with fine color in their purest forms, in modern times gemstones are identified by gemologists, who describe gems and their characteristics using technical terminology specific to the field of gemology. Gemstones are classified into different *groups*, *species*, and *varieties*. Gems characterized in terms of refractive index, dispersion, specific gravity and luster.

Just as scientist and gemologist characterize and classify gems, men do the same with the women they seek to court, date or marry.

Researchers say that the distinction in gemstones reflects the rarity of the respective stones as well as, their quality. The terminology that gemologist utilize to determine its characteristics is a resemblance of how most men observe women. The first characteristic a gemologist uses to identify a gemstone is its chemical composition. I stated above gemstones are classified into groups, species, and varieties by refractive index, dispersion, specific gravity and luster. To get a more in depth look at how a Jewel Expert views the gems he will transform into jewels I have broken this method down into specifics so that you may be familiar with my handbook of how to become a jewel expert.

Chemical Composition=Internal Compatibility:
Understanding the chemical composition (Her internal structure, principles, morals, etc.) of the gem you are looking to become a jewel will assist you in determining the foundational makeup of the type of women you pursue. If she does not possess the necessary analytical chemistry, the likely hood of the two of you encompassing the same goals for any type of relationship is highly unlikely.

Refractive Index=Refinery: Refining is the process that you utilize to fine tune the gem as it goes through the process of becoming your jewel. This process must include your care and concern, methods to dissect issues and render solutions, strong communication, dedication, loyalty and commitment.

Dispersion=Transformation: All healthy relationships must encompass a substantial dose of receptive communication. Being able to articulate your feelings, concerns, and thoughts in a concrete and concise manner is vital to the growth or failure of any relationship. This strong line of communication will allow transformation from being broken to sustaining long-term relationships with understanding, clarity and insight!

Rarity is another characteristic that lends value to a gemstone. When something is rare, it becomes more precious and valuable because of its uniqueness. God has offered us breathtaking gemstones that are desirable for their amazing beauty all over the world. The rarity, durability and value of these gemstones make them a remarkable asset enjoyed for generations.

Value

What is your value? This is one question I am not sure many evaluate in life or relationships. I bought my first car in 1996, it was a 1993 Honda Accord LX and I valued the car until I realized the dealership did not care, as much about the customer service they rendered when I was a potential customer versus when I actually became a buyer. I left my advertising job a year or so after, I purchased my car and fell behind on the payments. The bank that issued my loan began to call in search of payment and after a few hide the car at a friend's house attempts grew tiring, I finally allowed them to repossess the vehicle.

I realized years later that I did not value my new car as much as I originally thought because I failed to do what was necessary to maintain possession. When you truly care about something, you will do what is necessary to maintain the proper nurturing essential to increasing its value. I believe many men and women are often negligent in discovering what they are worth individually that they cannot appropriately ascertain their value as a couple or the value of the relationship. I asked at the top of this section a thought provoking question and below I will break down the jewel categories. Note that in the world of jewels their value is determined by the four C's- Color, Cut, Clarity and Crystal.

The Four Precious Stones:

Diamond- a diamond is renowned as a material with superlative physical qualities, has the highest hardness, and remarkable optical characteristics. It is the most popular gemstone transparent almost flawless and when cut and polished, valued as a precious gem

Diamonds are considered a girl's best friend. So many men go after Ms. Diamond because she is the most popular in the crowd and commands attention from everyone in the room. Although diamonds are the most popular they are also overused and appear egotistical because many of them lack flaws and because of their treatment by suitors, often consider themselves important therefore, may work less to impress you, care for your needs or improve the overall status of the relationship because of the imperfections it believes it possess.

Sapphire- A sapphire is prized for its translucent beauty. It is the focal point of many pieces of fine jewelry. They are easy to care for and virtually indestructible.

Ms. Sapphire is the cousin to Ms. Diamond and although they are related, she may not possess the same attitude or character flaws. They have always loomed in the shadow of the most popular woman in the room but hold the crown for being the most beautiful. The Sapphire woman understands her value and she may at times display a narcissistic attitude because of her unique beauty but, she also will care for you and in return be easy to care for as well.

Emerald- most emeralds are highly included, so their toughness (resistance to breakage) classifies as generally poor. A fine emerald must possess not only a pure luxuriant green hue but also a high degree of transparency for consideration as a top gem.

When you meet Ms. Emerald, you must pay attention to her self-esteem. She has a tendency to break easily because of her experiences and her lack of self worth. She is a luxuriant gem who is transparent at times to a fault but if you possess the tenacity to keep her empowered is worth the investment.

Ruby- The brightest and most valuable ruby is the "red" called pigeon blood red, commands a huge premium over other rubies of similar quality. The ruby is distinctive because of its unique color and deemed premium because of its clarity, cut and carat.

Ms. Ruby Red has a bright distinctive personality and often times stand out because of her angelic glow. Although she normally travels with a group of other women, she ranks over them because she has a deep understanding for what you will need and how to care for you.

The Honorable Mentions:

Pearl- a smooth, hard object produced within a soft shell tissue that contains a protective coating. The most valuable pearls are rare and spontaneous in the wild.

Ms. Pearl appears hardcore but underneath her tough exterior, she longs to be loved and has a soft heart. She is very spontaneous and in today's culture, she is very rare. You will enjoy discovering her and growing in a fruitful relationship.

Tanzanite- Tanzanite's known for their remarkable strong ability to resemble sapphire blue, violet and burgundy. They can also appear differently under alternate lighting. It requires artificial treatment.

Ms. Tanzanite blends in like a chameleon to hide her true flaws and very seldom display her original personality. She requires a great deal to care for because of her high superficial expectations and often will display her identity well into a relationship with a high investment.

During your quest to discover a jewel you must be careful of the counterfeits and imposters. You will be able to determine counterfeit jewels by their ability to handle high pressure.

You must also be on the lookout for jewel thieves. They are wolves dressed in sheep clothing disguising themselves as genuine concerned jewels who only desire to kill, steal and destroy. They aim to kill your dreams and ambition, steal your time and money and destroy your character and self-worth.

Treatments and Enhancements

Improving the quality of gemstones by treating them is common practice for a jewel expert. Applying the proper care to the gems you discover is the key to enhancing its overall beauty, increasing its value and ensuring its long-term care. I often say you cannot treat a Mercedes as you would a Honda. The vehicles have different care plans that cause them to be distinctively separate although they both are vehicles. If maintained properly a Mercedes can last you a very long time but its maintenance is expensive. A Honda may be easier to obtain and care for because its costs are considerably lower but you cannot place a Mercedes emblem on a Honda and call it a Benz.

Whatever gem you decide to pursue learning and understanding its care package plan is essential to progression. Being well informed will assist you in properly providing its necessities. The journey ahead is challenging but bright and you have the tools necessary to be successful.

THE CLOSER 45

The end of a thing is far greater than the beginning...You cannot get to your promised land without beginning your Exodus.

American actress Kyra Sedgwick starred on the TNT crime drama "The Closer", in which she played Deputy Chief Brenda Leigh Johnson, a police detective who often closes her cases using sometimes questionable yet very effective methods. In baseball, a closing pitcher, more frequently referred to as a closer, is a relief pitcher that specializes in closing out games. I admire the police detective and the baseball pitcher because they each have a goal to complete an assignment. Most importantly, in completing the assignment, they each utilize their designation of a team; either the police force or the athletes on the baseball field. This insures that the task is completed.

Becoming an effective closer will require extensive training, keen focus, efficient follow through and masterful tools. As you journey into the realm of more healthy relationships remember the following:

- **Show no fear** –Do not be afraid to venture into unchartered territory.

- **No commission selling-** Be genuine in your approach. Do not come across like a used car salesperson selling for commissions.
- **Understand that prospects have doubts & fears-** Many of the women you encounter may have bruises from previous relationships allow time for a connection and a conversation flow and disarm your mate by reaffirming.
- **Become immune to rejection-** In your searches you may encounter many agony dates of disconnect before finding your jewel; be patient with the process.
- **Avoid all negative influences and distractions-** Stay committed and focused on the objective.
- **Stay competitive yet stress free-** Compete only with yourself and your goals. Keep records of your progress but never compete against others for a mate. Your unique personality will align you with the suitable mate.

Looking at 2nd Before Landing on 1st

The expression in baseball is *never look at second base before you land on first base.* This allows you to focus on one-step or action at a time without getting ahead of the game. When a player looks to steal a base before he secures his footing, he eliminates himself from the possibilities of scoring. Dating has turned into a smorgasbord of who can sleep with the most individuals; as if dating is a competition and its participants are aiming for the record books. The key to actively progressing with a healthy dialogue is going at the pace of the woman you are pursuing. Allow her to dictate what happens in the relationship and at what pace. Looking to marry or discussing marriage before you get to know one another is relationship suicide and often times will turn a woman off. Talking about things that are too advanced for the status of the relationship can be discouraging as well. Exercising extreme patience and allowing the relationship to materialize is very important to understanding the dynamics of your unique relationship and developing the proper utensils to accommodate the relationship moving forward.

Five Basic Survival Skills

One of the most important elements to survival is between your ears - your brain. **DO NOT PANIC**, use your wits and practice all elements of the Five Basics in your relationship before you need to rely on them.

FIRE- In terms of camping survival a fire can purify water, cook food, signal rescuers, provide warmth, light and comfort, help keep predators at a distance, and, can be a most welcome friend and companion. Each person who ventures into the elements of dating should have a minimum of two ways to start a fire in that relationship. A few small fires along the journey of dating will keep the flame burning once you have been together for a while. When the two of you bring your individual fires into the relationship, it will create a large fire that ignites your love for one another. Collect firewood and fuel to keep predators away from your exclusive bond. Make reflectors while dating that will remind you of why you fell in love with your mate and how you can restart the fires that may have extinguished during the course of the relationship.

SHELTER- Is the means by which you protect your body from excess exposure to the sun, cold, wind, rain or snow during outdoor survival. Providing a place of shelter for your mate is crucial in times of doubt or drought. Your mate must know at all times that you will protect them from the elements of society. **Ephesians 6:11-18** says,

Put on the full armor of God so that you can take your stand against the devil's schemes. For our struggle is not against flesh and blood, but against the rulers, against the authorities, against the powers of this dark world and against the spiritual forces of evil in the heavenly realms. Therefore put on the full armor of God, so that when the day of evil comes, you may be able to stand your ground, and after you have done everything, to stand. Stand firm then, with the belt of truth buckled around your waist, with the breastplate of righteousness in place, and with your feet fitted with the readiness that comes from the gospel of peace. an addition to all this, take up the shield of faith, with which you can extinguish all the flaming arrows of the evil one. Take the helmet of salvation and the sword of the Spirit, which is the word of God. And pray in the Spirit on all occasions with all kinds of prayers and requests. With this in mind, be alert and always keep on praying for all the saints.

SIGNALING –Create an effective communication system that will allow the two of you to efficiently alert one another when you have issues, problems or concerns. This will eliminate any possibility for outside influence to divide your household.

FOOD / WATER- These elements are vital towards your survival. The body cannot function properly without the essential nutrients needed to operate at its optimum level. What you feed each other will determine how you grow and develop as a couple. Feed negativity or energy deficient liquids to one another and the relationship will respond with sluggish performances, excess fat, and poisonous chatter.

FIRST AID- Administering first aid to your relationship when necessary will almost single handedly insure its survival. When you or your mate are injured, either emotionally or physically, having the ability to dispense suitable care will guarantee longevity and allot healing.

Adapt or Die

Adapting in life allows room for growth and development. Relationships are all about adapting to the environment that is present versus the one presented at an earlier time. Most people feel as though compromising is a form of adaption, I disagree. Adapting is making suitable adjustments to the requirements or conditions, while compromising is settling and making concessions to differences. You can adapt without compromising but you cannot compromise without adapting. When we refuse to adapt to the growth or decline of relationships that relationship is now in jeopardy of dying.

Skydiving without a Parachute

Who would willingly exit an aircraft in an attempt to return to earth without the aid of a parachute? Skydiving is typically done at an altitude of 3,000 to 13,000 feet. Experts consider skydiving with a parachute risky and dangerous. Jumping from an airplane (**having sex**) without a parachute (**a condom or protection**), relying on specially designed wind suits or your equipment and skills (**your manhood and limited sexual skills**) increases your risk fatality (**disease and death**). People are jumping into risky sex planes (**relationships**) without the proper aid to ensure a safe landing. If you decide to have sex at any point in your relationship with a mate who is not your husband or wife be sure to take precaution and protect yourself and your mate.

Text vs. Call

Scenario: Meet a girl…like a girl…approach a girl…exchange phone numbers with a girl…and then the first interaction…you text a girl. *****WRONG*****

Your first interaction with a woman that you have an interest should not be via text message. The message you send with a text message first versus a phone call is you have a superficial approach to getting to know her. You must come out of the gate with your best foot forward. Texting is very impersonal for an initial conversation and does not say much about her value to you. Be sure your initial communication with the woman you have a keen interest in dating is one that speaks volumes about you, your intentions and, her worth to you. She will appreciate your approach and reward you throughout the relationship.

Missing the Homerun

I once heard a story about a minor league baseball catcher name Jeremy Brown, who while playing for the Visalia Oaks a Class A team of the Arizona Diamondbacks, hit a homerun but did not recognize he had done so. Brown, who weighed two hundred and forty pounds, was scared to run to second base. In one game, a fast pitch is thrown to Jeremy and he hits the ball to deep center field. He does what he has never done before, he goes for it and attempts to round first base but falls down; he scrambles to make it back to first base before being thrown out. His team and the fans begin to laugh at him, and he soon would find out why. Jeremy realized at that very moment that the ball went sixty feet over the fence. He hit a homerun and did not realize it. We often view the wrong definition of success and in the process miss what matters most. Being caught up in society's definition of what you or your relationship should look like will distract you from seeing the success you have had over the years and although the relationship may have ended, you were victorious. Comparing and contrasting your relationship with that of others will thrust you into a competitive nature depleting the foundation you built with your spouse and cause you to feel inadequate attempting to measure up to superficial expectations.

Embracing God's standard for success will empower you to revolutionize your life and relationship and place you in a position of authority over the things that once held you back from giving of yourself and receiving from others. Keep your eyes on the ball and do not lose sight of it in the lights of dating, expectations and lust. You are fully equipped to love yourself and move past the trauma you may have experienced in previous relationships. There is no limit to the experiences you will have moving forward but be sure you are able to recognize the homeruns you will hit in life and celebrate every triumphant step you take toward total healing, restoration and empowerment.

PART SEVEN: HER JEWELS

⏻ Power Point to Ponder

Understanding what assets and liabilities are will be the key to growing productive and healthy relationships. Treating your mate with the proper respect, discovering the true gems, and adopting consistent habits of self-evaluation will afford you the opportunity to become a Treasure Hunter who will eventually become a true Jewel Expert.

❓ Question to Consider

Are you looking for a substitute to replace your voids? Have you carefully examined the pros and cons to your new adventure? Are you the man she will essentially desire? How do you continue to improve your character, integrity and overall being?

💎 Jewel Tip

Do not allow what others do measure what you will do.

POWER NOTES:

CONCLUSION

I pray that this book has provided clear understanding about how you approach the relationship with yourself as well as how to build healthy effective relationships with others. Though many may tell you that the after affects of previous relationships only last a few weeks or months it is very possible that if the injury has gone undetected can last for years.

You have the power to change the thermostat of your life. Be strategic and tactful in your approach and never allow someone with no power to your destiny influence your journey.

Your destiny waits with more to offer than your past, embrace it and run into it with joy, peace and laughter. Life and love does not have to be complicated if we learn to adapt to the environment, adopt a winning attitude, design a winning model, devise a winning strategy, devote to a training regiment and execute the proper mechanics.

I pray that you become the man that God designed you to be and in doing so allow healing to your heart, restoration within your manhood and an empowering spirit to engulf your soul. God has fuel left in the tank for you. I encourage you to **Keep Running** toward your purpose and cross the finish line in victory.

REFERENCES

Anna Driver and Eileen O'Grady, Rueters | Yahoo Finance 2012

Victoria Duff | budgeting.thenest.com 2011

Infidelity Facts | infidelityfacts.com 2009

Jennifer Walker | ehow.com 2012

The Daily Beast | thedailybeast.com

Wikipedia | Wikipedia.com

AUTHOR BIOGRAPHY

Mo Stegall, is a world class keynote speaker, prominent relationship expert and empowerment coach. His empowering platform has encouraged and transformed millions of lives worldwide. He is passionately inspired to educate, encourage, and empower communities globally.

He travels the country teaching men how to become *Treasure Hunters* & *Jewel Experts*, assisting women identify their strengths and deficiencies with his popular *Jewel Tips* and empowers communities to build healthy relationships through his widely successful *Power Talks*.

A visionary, pioneer and journeyman, Mo Stegall transcends any medium he touches. Clients call him "The Treasure Hunter" because of his ability to empower people to discover their inner jewels and gems. He is a global humanitarian who once was homeless, endured the loss of his mother to AIDS, and experienced several life setbacks but has championed his journey and dedicated his life to serving others. Mr. Stegall focuses on teaching individuals the importance of self-discovery, how to maneuver through adverse situations, and gives practical steps to achieving life goals. He offers proportional doses of Vitamin E, which stands for EMPOWERMENT.

He has assisted with missions abroad including putting shoes in underserved communities with the Samaritans Feet Organization in Lima, Peru. He has empowered college students to take control of their financial destiny alongside acclaimed actor and bestselling author Hill Harper on the UNCF HBCU Empower Me Tour. He challenged a nation to get involved with education, employment, housing, and health-care as Youth Empowerment Ambassador for the National Urban League's I Am Empowered campaign.

He has served as host of the Auburn University Healthy Relationships Summit, Bishop Paul Morton's Full Gospel Baptist Conference, The Bank of America Show ME Karma Teen Summit and the Georgia Gubernatorial Debate. He is also an advocate for Empowering Women to discover their inner jewel.

As a Brand Ambassador he has represented various corporations and brands such as Ford, Wachovia, UNCF, National Urban League and many others. He has been the voice image for many products and services and has been heard on television and radio commercials across the nation for Acura, Best Buy, Hitachi, Radio One, Delta, NBC, ESPN, GA Lottery, Oakwood and Georgia Power, to name a few.

His drive and tenacity allows him to passionately approach projects and assignments while his "serving others first" mentality and warm personality invites people of all ages and backgrounds into his disarming circle with ease.

He has worked with the Special Olympics and various school systems in support of the Anti-Bullying campaign.

He serves in a variety of capacities and with a number of community organizations including Celebrity Ambassador for Operation Hope's Banking On Our Future & 5MK Initiatives as well as Entertainment Ambassador for Samaritan's Feet Barefoot for Barefeet campaign.

He is the founder and president of the I Can Be Foundation Inc., a 501c3 organization dedicated to improving communities through various empowerment tools and programs.

Mo Stegall is a popular conference speaker, event emcee and college lecturer. To learn more, you can visit www.mostegall.com

OTHER PRODUCTS FROM MO STEGALL

Against All Odds I Can Be 10 Steps To Revolutionize Your Destiny:

Against All Odds I Can Be is the empowering best-selling book by Mo Stegall. *Against All Odds I Can Be* was voted **#1 Hot New Release** by Amazon and named One of the Most Inspiring and Powerful Books released last year by Celebrity Magazine.

This book will show you, step-by-step how to discover your worth, overcome adversity, and achieve goals!

This book is essential to anyone that has a quest for success. In this book you have the blueprint it could be considered a motivational bible of sort.

--**Dennis White**, Actor/Acting Coach/Producer

Poetic Language: When the Heart Speaks Book

The book that empowers the heart while loving the soul, educates the mind while encouraging the spirit.

A powerful collection of poems by Mo Stegall empowering men and women to explore their inner beauty.

Poetic Language When The Heart Speaks CD: The highly anticipated poetry album from bestselling author Mo Stegall. This electrifying CD will captivate your heart, stimulate your mind, and refresh your soul. Stegall's delivery with every track coupled with the thunderous musical production makes this album a must have. The album also includes a few bonus tracks with his collaboration with Jazz great Walt J and gospel hip-hop artist Hood (John P. Kee, BB Jay, Mary Mary)

Power Talks with Mo Stegall is a series of powerful, inspiring and entertaining messages designed to educate, encourage and empower listeners to take control and revolutionize their destinies. Enjoy these impactful messages.

- 5 Power Steps to Emerging from the Pack
- 7 Keys to Removing Obstacles That Prohibit Growth
- How to Be Patient with Your Dreams
- How To Discover Your Worth When You Feel Worthless
- How To Get The Best In You Out of You
- How To Unlock The Chambers of Fear & Succeed
- Power Steps To Achieving Your Goals
- Bonus: The Ram in the Bush Power Pill

Also get Mo Stegall's Empowering Apparel

Empowering Messages with Innovative Designs

Plus Many More: Log on to www.mostegall.com